S P A C E

space /spās/ n. [L. spatium] - 1. the unlimited three-dimensional realm or expanse in which all material objects are located and all events occur. 2. The portion or extent of this in a given instance. 3. extent or area in two dimensions; a particular extent of surface. [...]

BODIES

```
bod·y /bod'e/ n., pl. bod·ies (OE bodig). [...] - 1. the
physical structure and material substance of an
animal, plant, or other organism 6. (physics. a mass,
esp. one considered a whole. 9. a collective group.
12. substance: consistency or richness. 13. the basic
material of which a ceramic is made. [...]
```

FIGURES

```
fig·ure /fig'yer/ n. [L figura "shape, trope =
fig- (base of fingere "to shape") + ura"]. [...]
5. the form or shape of something; outline. 6. The
bodily form or frame: "a graceful figure." [...]
9. a representation, pictorial or sculptured, esp.
of the human form. [...]
```

Gianluca Peluffo
Valerio Paolo Mosco

Space, **Bodies**, Figures
A genealogy for Peluffo & Partners' Architecture

This book came to be through a collaboration between an architect and a critic. It came out of the fact that both the architect and the critic share a good number of things. Not everything, but certainly a lot. The architect and the critic compared ideas about exactly what it is that draws them together and out of this discussion came a work that evolved somewhat on its own.

The method through which the discussion took place was a venerable one, based on images or, better, on their analogical juxtaposition. The architect proposed images of his projects, putting them in relation with others that came mostly from Italian artistic tradition. The projects had been designed and built over the course of the years with the associates of Peluffo & Partners (Paola De Lucia, Domenico Faraco, Gabriele Filippi, and Antonio Lagorio, formerly with 5+1) or in association with 5+1AA, Rudy Ricciotti, Orazio Carpenzano, Stefano Pujatti, and Beniamino Servino. They were illustrated time and again by photographs taken by Ernesta Caviola, who has always collaborated on fine-tuning what is now, to use a term from times past, the style of Peluffo & Partners.

The architect shared analogical juxtapositions with the critic, who in turn emended them engendering a dialogue that sought what held the images together. There were links that initially appeared immediate yet over time seemed elusive, but then again every—even the most banal—analogical juxtaposition is always enigmatic and in the most interesting cases even mysterious. At the start, the purpose of the dialogue was not at all clear. The whole thing seemed like a game that could have gone on forever, but neither of them felt they were wasting time. Time is never lost looking at images, playing with their infinite analogies; it actually seems to be regenerated, even prolonged through the analogical game of images. Playing with the juxtapositions, adding phrases that also came out by analogy, it became increasing clear that, without explicit intention, the architect and the critic were trying to structure a language—structuring in the sense of making it more solid, more necessary to itself.

The critic was a bit disoriented. Working in this way he was no longer a critic, he was no longer making judgments from the outside, a posteriori. By playing with the juxtapositions and commenting on them with the architect, he was becoming an accomplice to the latter's choices; he was turning into a sort of music producer, a figure who gives advice, who comments on the piece trying to help the authors see it differently. This sort of work is quite rare in a postmodernity that breeds two categories of critics. The first are the moralists, who, well sheltered from choice, judge works a posteriori, most often to tear them apart, thereby contributing to the nihilism that increasingly confines architecture in its irrelevance. Their irreverence is contrasted by the commercial acquiescence of the second category of critics, whose ambition is nothing more than becoming the officiants of the increasingly weary rites of current cultural regimes. Wreckers versus celebrants therefore, two dangerous breeds, beyond which it was necessary to find a third way. Both the critic and the architect were convinced of this.

For the two of them, the hypothesis of how to operate became defined as the work progressed. Considering the results as a whole, the method used—the analogical juxtaposition of images— gave rise to what the architect insisted on calling a "genealogy." Every image referred to another in a filiation that was not chronological but mixed the eras in a somewhat lighthearted way so that fathers, mothers, grandfathers, grandmothers, children, grandchildren, and great-grandchildren all lived together, as in the banquet of Aeolus to which Ulysses had been invited. Memory clearly goes back to Aby Warburg's suggestive and extravagant juxtapositions, but there was a substantial difference between his juxtapositions and the ones the two proposed. In his analogical juxtapositions, Warburg actually hypothesized involving the whole universe, therein pursuing the titanic idea of giving rise to a genealogy of images that would transcend time and space. What the architect and the critic hypothesized was far less ambitious. They definitely intended to transcend time, demonstrating therein a deliberate indifference to chronology, but they were not at all intent on transcending space. The images they chose actually have the characteristic of belonging to a well-defined physical space, to a very specific country: to Italy, the country they are both from and in which they both live. So if the images wander through time, they are conversely well rooted in space, and it is this rootedness that makes it possible to speak expressly of genealogy.

What was it that held together the different images of Italian art to which Peluffo & Partners' projects sought to refer? Three themes, basically: the body, space, and the figure. Let's start with the body. From the very beginning the Christian matrix of Italian figurative culture, implanted in the Middle Ages in the sediment of classical naturalism, had established the body, primarily the human body, as the main object of representation. Looking closely however, not just one but actually three bodies seem to live in parallel in Italian art, at times hybridizing with each other. The first is the suffering, sometimes even despairing earthly body: Mary Magdalene's body in Masaccio's *Crucifixion* or the many bodies clinging to their own drama in Caravaggio's paintings. The second is the spiritualized body, the body that is still earthly but has discovered divinity through the intercession of the Holy Spirit. These are Beato Angelico's and Piero della Francesca's bodies, bodies that are suspended in an intermediate state as if poised between two realms, that of the heavens and that of the earth. Finally, there is the resurrected body. Christianity is the only religion that actually postulates the resurrection of bodies from death, and it was this now entirely metaphysical state, so beautifully described in Dante Alighieri's "Paradise," that was the obsession of fourteenth- and fifteenth-century Italian painting. By analogy, these three different states correspond to the Trinity and describe a progression from the immanent realistic figurativeness of the body "on the ground" to the abstraction of the resurrected body now part of the Kingdom of Heaven. These three bodies hold together the vast spectrum in which Italian figurative culture has been expressed, its corporal genealogy and, with it, its intrinsic drama. This was well understood by Lionello Venturi, Roberto Longhi, Giovanni Testori, and Pier Paolo Pasolini. It was also understood by some modern artists, such as Lucio Fontana, who struggled lifelong between these three interpretations, in a real conflict with the body, denying it, exalting it, depicting it as pure matter, or abstracting it into the celestial dimension.

The second vertex of this hypothetical Italian genealogy is represented by space. In artistic and especially in architectural representation, the isolated body is incomplete, as though it needs a space around it that can contain it and bring out its expressive potential. With classical Greco-Roman art, body and space began a long dialogue that, despite today's increasingly miserable attempts to deny it, corresponds to Western representation's *raison d'être*. In preceding eras, body and space came together or took distance from each other, sometimes even going so far as to turn their backs on each other. Italian architecture has given masterful evidence of this complex relationship between body and space, to the extent that it can be said that the genealogy of Italian architecture is actually based on the staging of the figure in space—a space that is ideal as well as physical and, in its greatest moments, ideal and physical at the same time. Like all Italian forms of expression, the staging of the body in space has varied. In Giuseppe Perugini, Nello Aprile, and Mario Fiorentino's Mausoleum of the Fosse Ardeatine, as well as Giovanni Michelucci's Church of the Autostrada, it has privileged touch. In other circumstances, such as Giuseppe Terragni's Casa del Fascio and Luigi Moretti's Fencing Academy, it has privileged visual perception. In still other rare, invaluable cases, it has tried to hold these two perceptions together, as in Ignazio Gardella's Padiglione di Arte Moderna in Milan.

The figure, the last vertex of the genealogical triangle, can be seen as the derivative of the relationship between body and space. In and of itself the relationship between body and space does not exist; it appears when it is represented, when it becomes a figure. If we consider the works of Paolo Cavallini, Giotto, Beato Angelico, Piero della Francesca, and, more generally, of all the artists that Lionello Venturi called the "Italian primitives," it is evident that the overall image is created by the cohabitation of the figures, be they human or architectural, in the space that contains them. The result is a refined hybridization: the human bodies become partly architectural and the architectural bodies partly human. This interdependence is what engenders the fascination of these representations on which the proposed genealogy is based.

Body, space, and figure, therefore, are the vertices of the genealogical triangle within which to seek how something is done or, rather, the characteristics of style. It is a limited genealogical triangle that is quite aware being such, that has the flaw of being completely *arcitaliano,* a word Curzio Malaparte used to summarize all that is Italian. These three terms, therefore, have to be seen from an "Italian" perspective and, as such, not in contradiction but inextricably linked through the most inclusive of rhetorical figures, the chiasmus. The chiasmus is a symbol of an a-dual worldview, opposed to any form of Manichaeism. To the architect and the critic, the either/or, the Protestant or Calvinist that characterizes Nordic figurative culture and by extension the modern architecture pertaining to it, seemed to be the negation of the hypothesized genealogical triangle. Yet that Nordic, tendentially iconoclastic figurative culture, which still nourishes most of today's Western figurative culture, has had the advantage of being the contrasting agent that has made Italian genealogy more evident. Moreover, as both the architect and the critic noted, Italy—its history, its facts, and its art—cannot be seen through dualism; it has never worked. As Francesco Guicciardini had already understood in the sixteenth century, Italian languages are based on inclusion, if not hybridization, and the law that moves them is metamorphosis—the even imperceptible, degree-by-degree transformation of individual facts, individual actors, and individual figures. Are Giotto's paintings sacred or profane? Are Bernini's sculptures chaste or immodest? Is Michelucci's architecture modern or not? Is Terragni abstract or figurative? We could go on until today. The fact remains that as the architect and critic proceeded in their work, they gradually became convinced that in the moment in which Italian art and architecture had strayed from a-duality, when they had undermined the inclusive character of their worldview, they had lost their way, leaving behind irrelevant, if not damaging, traces.

To recount the "arch-Italian" genealogy of Peluffo & Partners' work, to narrate the story of its lineage and its implications through somewhat daring and even somewhat heretical juxtapositions, the architect and the critic have relied upon what they call four "actions." They have organized the sequence of juxtapositions through these four actions—through revealing, evoking, transfiguring, sharing—adding a theme that recurs more or less subtly in Peluffo & Partners' projects and that, with a certain whimsy, they have defined as "clumsiness." In extreme synthesis, these actions and theme follow.

- ***Revealing***

The desire and the need for architecture that makes itself visible, that has the courage to make itself visible. A non-reticent, talkative architecture that does not stop at communication alone, that involves everyone experiencing it physically. A revealing that is visual, tactile, figurative, and spatial.

- ***Evoking***

The desire and the need for architecture that has a long narrative that does not stop at a slogan or catchphrase. An architecture that is predisposed to narration through a metaphorical language that can generate other figures and other images, or if nothing else evoke them.

- ***Transfiguring***

The need for architecture that does not invent extraordinary objects, that does not become design, that has the capacity to transfigure even anonymous building elements into something that, with necessary prudence, can approach the extraordinary.

-    ***Sharing***

The need to express itself through a language that is predisposed to being shared. A language that is popular but not populist, that does not bend to the presumed wishes, aspirations, or frustrations of the masses. A language that is capable of transforming communication into sharing.

-    ***Clumsiness***

A means of expression in which everything does not necessarily add up, in which the elements, in their configuration and the way they relate to each other, always maintain a certain "clumsy" irregularity. The Futurists' anti-gracefulness is to be replaced by the more docile figure of clumsiness, by a form that can keep grace and anti-gracefulness in balance.

For the architect and the critic, these four actions and the theme of clumsiness might engender what they call a "meta-language"—a generous, certainly not unflawed language; a language that, if compared to many of today's trends appears quite dated, or if nothing else nonaligned. It is not aligned with the polished, aseptic, wholly a-corporal compactness of design architecture. It is not aligned with iconic minimal architecture, with that non-referential, tendentially aseptic architecture that is so fashionable in Northern Europe today. And it is not aligned with socially or ecologically well-intended architecture that reduces architecture's magnificent semantic complexity to cheap slogans.

To conclude and to continue, the authors entrust the reader to Umberto Boccioni's plea: "Let's throw ourselves wide open to the space and enclose the figure!"

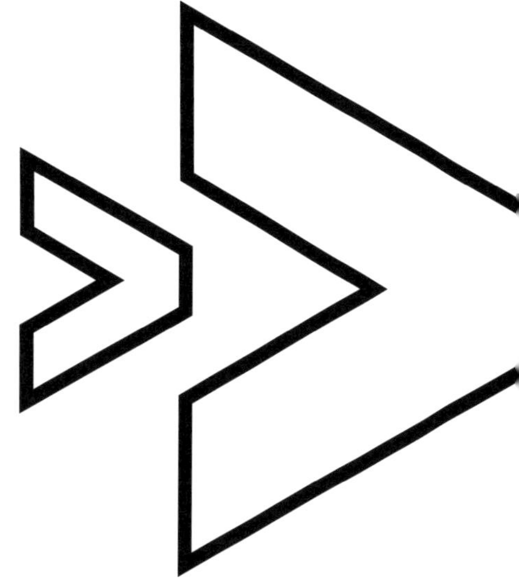

Revealing

re•veal (ri vel') v.t [L _revelare_ to unveil] - 1. to make known; disclose; divulge: "to reveal a secret." 2. to lay open to view; display; exhibit.

From *Random House Webster's College Dictionary*

Thoughts and forms can be divided into two families: thoughts and forms that are conceived to be revealed, and thoughts and forms that are conceived to stay hidden. What is of interest here is first of these two families: architecture that is transitive, that "speaks" and, as such, has no qualms about making itself visible. Architecture that "speaks" has one characteristic: it is intelligible, it tends toward clarity, presenting itself in such a way that anyone who sees or experiences it can grasp it with immediacy. Intelligibility does not mean that what is made visible is completely accessible and thus easily consumable. Clarity does not necessarily impose banality; on the contrary, intelligibility sometimes has something mysterious about it. In his essay on Piero della Francesca, Roberto Longhi wrote about the "mystery of maximum visibility," the mystery that is celebrated in the moment it is revealed, as in Piero's frescoes in Arezzo. Hence architecture that "speaks," that makes itself visible. But what does it reveal? There are endless answers to this question, we chose one: genealogy. Stravinsky used to say that what is not quotation is plagiarism: it was clearly a boutade but one that nonetheless shows awareness of how every form of expression, even those that end up being the most radical and innovative, is indebted to past forms. In other words, every form, from those that are literary to those that are artistic, carries a genealogy within it. The author may or may not disavow this genealogy, which is most often unconscious, to the extent that authors themselves are often not aware of committing plagiarism. Revealing genealogy relies on the practically infinite series of references and analogies that a form necessarily carries within it. Genealogy roots architecture by making it necessary to itself, in a certain sense it makes it irreplaceable. Yet revealing is not a univocal act, it necessarily implies a relationship with someone who perceives it; if this were not so, it would be a sterile narcissism and nothing more. When one sees a work of value that has been made visible, something unexpected happens: what is perceived, in turn, looks back at us creating a chiasmus, a reciprocal interpenetration of the parts.

Communicating by revealing genealogy carries a risk: the risk of mannerism, namely, an affected didascalic appropriation and, with it, the haughtiness evident in the worst mannered works. The latter seem to communicate but ultimately they do not; they actually exalt themselves, often slipping into idolatry. Architecture that "speaks" and that knows how to make itself visible stops short of exaltation, it avoids quotation, it shuns idolatry. It knows the art of concealing the sources on which it feeds.

Revealing

There is an evident analogy between the statue of Marcus Aurelius on Capitoline Hill in Rome and the face Masaccio painted. Both are shown explicitly in a pose that is grave and serene, hieratic yet still completely human. For human beings, revealing oneself is a natural, even banal act, but just how one is revealed is a complex choice that defines a language and with it the character of a representation. Though made centuries apart, the face of Marcus Aurelius and the face portrayed by Masaccio disclose more than just themselves; they reveal their genealogy, their familiarity over the centuries—a long-lasting familiarity that emerges through the representation itself. The two faces are visibly open yet maintain their distance from onlookers. Everything is played out in the measure of this distance; it has to avoid too much familiarity and too much detachment.

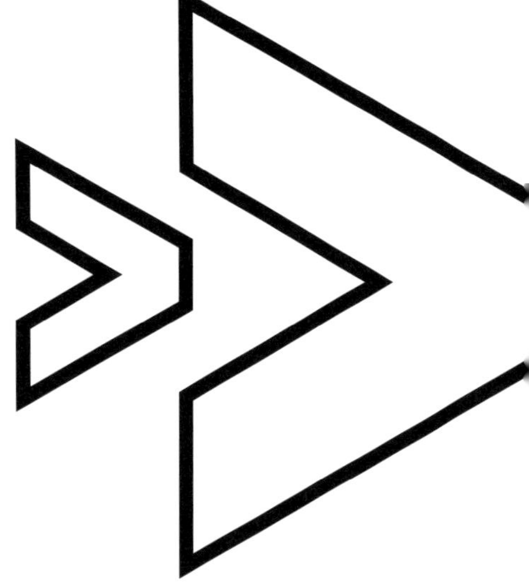

1. Statue of Marcus Aurelius,
   taken from "Arte Romana,"
   edited by Edoardo Persico in
   Domus, no. 96, 1935

2. Masaccio, *The Tribute
   Money*, detail of Saint Peter's
   face, 1423–28, Brancacci
   Chapel, church of Santa
   Maria del Carmine, Florence

1

Revealing

The fisherman depicted in the Greek fresco is showing off the fish he has caught. He is not portrayed at the moment in which he caught them, nor is it the moment in which the fish are lying in the market stall. The painter shows them in-between these two actions, in a particular moment that is both usual and unusual. The fisherman is depicted in a highly symbolic everyday act, so as to represent the Mediterranean marine civilization of which he is part. In the project for the Port of Trapani, the building objects—the pavilions and the overlying vaults—mean to be visible in a particular moment in which their belonging to everyday life is about to pass into the timeless representation of architecture. This moment coincides with its opposite: the moment in which architecture's timelessness is about to open up and accommodate everyday life.

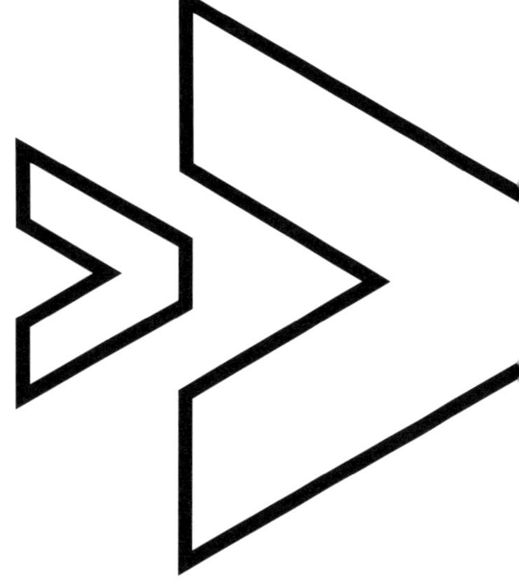

1. Project for Trapani's new
   waterfront, detail of the fish
   market, 2021

2. *Fresco of a Fisherman*,
   Museum of Prehistoric
   Thira, Santorini,
   1650–1500 BC

1

Revealing

In artistic representation the body can be revealed directly, in architecture a series of rhetorical figures are needed: analogy first and foremost, metaphor, synecdoche, metonymy, and even hyperbole. The body can be revealed by itself and/or in relation to other bodies. When two or three bodies are represented together, one in front of the other, there is a sense of witnessing a mute conversation between different architectures. It is a conversation between structures not statues, between objects that make themselves available to being experienced by people who will enter them, wander among them, experience them, and leave them. The project for the Italian Pavilion at Expo Dubai staged this conversation between bodies through pavilions surrounding a central empty space, which is bounded and defined by the architectural bodies around it. Without their presence the empty space they contain would vanish, as if swallowed up in itself. Modernity, alas, abounds in voids that have been sucked into themselves.

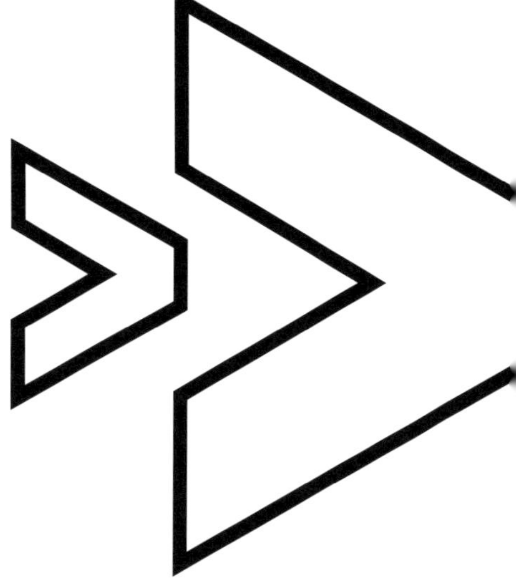

1. Project for the Italian
   Pavilion, Expo Dubai 2020

2. Arturo Martini, *The Dream*,
   terra-cotta high relief, 1931

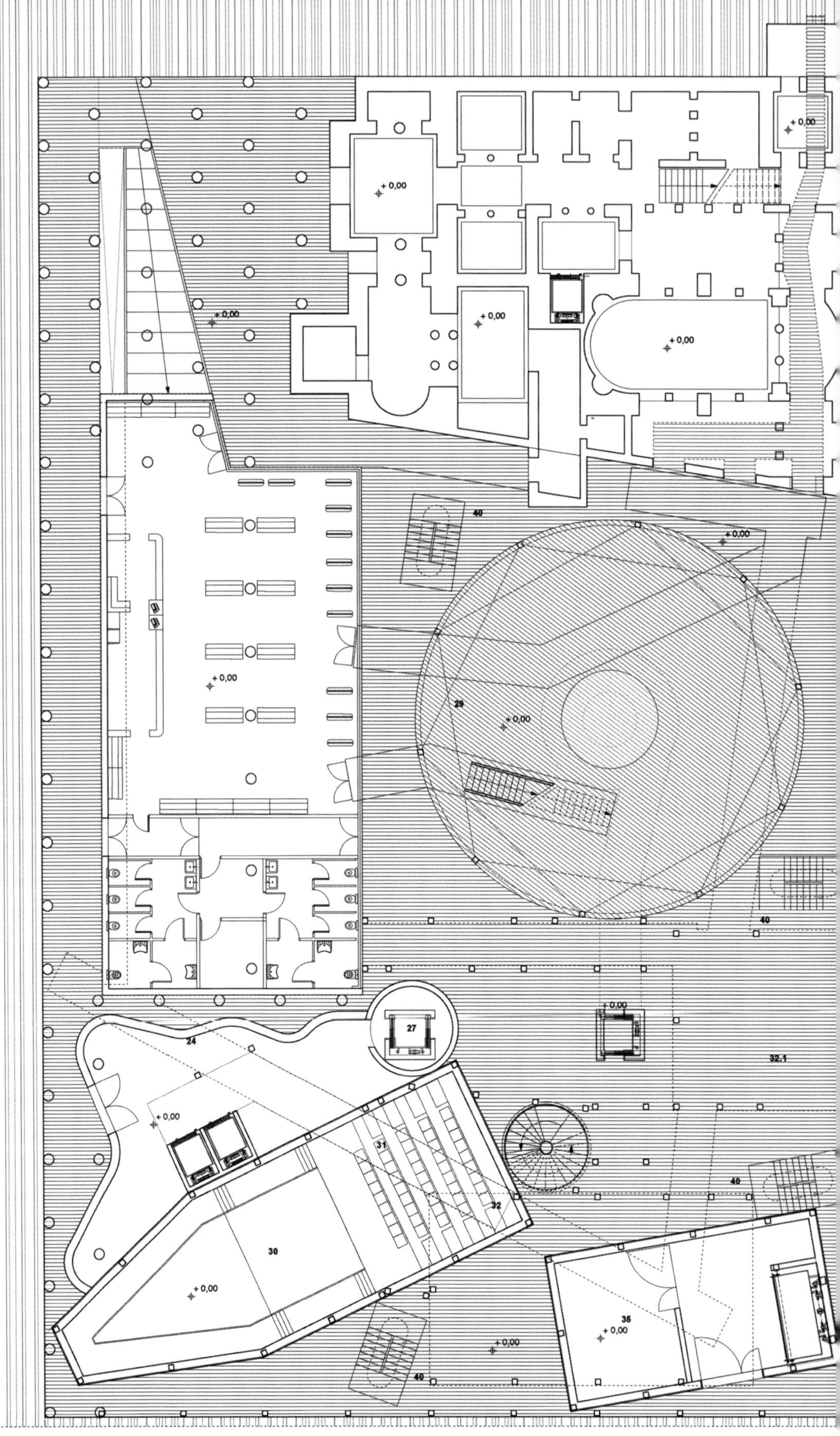

+ 0,00
+ 0,00
+ 0,00
+ 0,00
+ 0,00
+ 0,00
+ 0,00
+ 0,00
+ 0,00
+ 0,00
+ 0,00
+ 0,00
+ 0,00
40
40
40
40
40
29
24
27
30
31
32
32.1
35
1

Revealing

If we think of associating the verb "reveal" with architecture, we are reminded of the loquacious buildings that deliberately assert their presence in urban space—buildings with a well-defined character that are not at all elusive. In addition to this well-known approach to visibility there is another that is found in some of the interiors of Italian architecture. What comes to mind in this regard is the large hall of Luigi Moretti's Fencing Academy, which reveals itself to the extent of actually enveloping us. Yet it is not a solid space, it seems to be made of emptiness—an emptiness that makes itself visible in absolute whiteness. An enveloping, as if emulsified, whiteness wraps around us like an extremely rarified fog; a fog that, by analogy, is found in Emanuele Crialese's beautiful film *Golden Door* (original Italian title: *Nuovomondo*). It is the white that suspends the forms in the space making them intangible, like apparitions; and it is the white, through shades ranging from the absolute to the tactile, that reveals the quintessence of the space, what can be called its figurative structure.

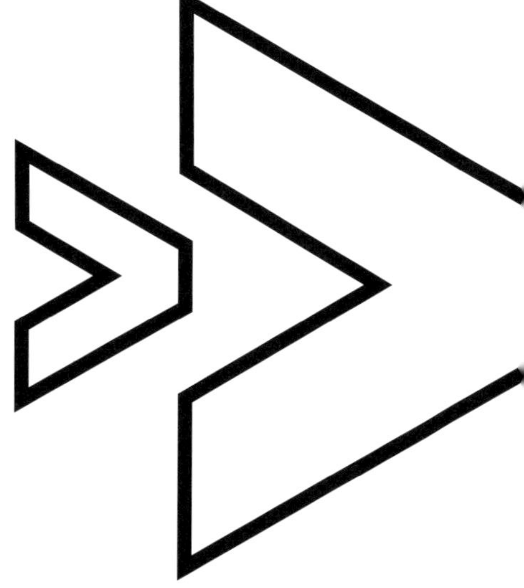

1. Emanuele Crialese,
   Golden Door, still frame,
   Italy, 2006

2. Reuse of ex-Caserma
   Ferdinando di Savoia –
   Ministero degli Interni,
   2015, Rome

Revealing

Revealing cannot do without hiding. The two terms do not form a dyad, yet one is necessary to the other. In Shakespeare's *As You Like it*, the melancholy Jacques hides in the Forest of Arden: his hiding amplifies and, on his sudden appearance, makes the monologues more lively. Just a few signs of the museum project for the Battle of El Alamein in the Egyptian desert appear outside on the ground over which the tower-landmark looms. These few signs are traces, if not clues, of the interior spatial richness; the landmark is the device that signals the monument on the desert horizon. Melville wrote that "calm is but the wrapper and the envelope of the storm." The same could be said about the space: its negation is the wrapper, the envelope that encloses its richness.

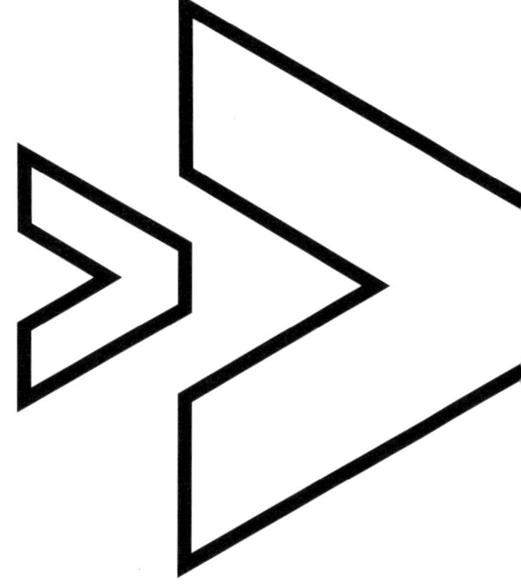

1. Project for the El Alamein
   Battle Museum 2018, Egypt

2. Lucio Fontana emerging
   from the trapdoor of his
   studio with André Verdet

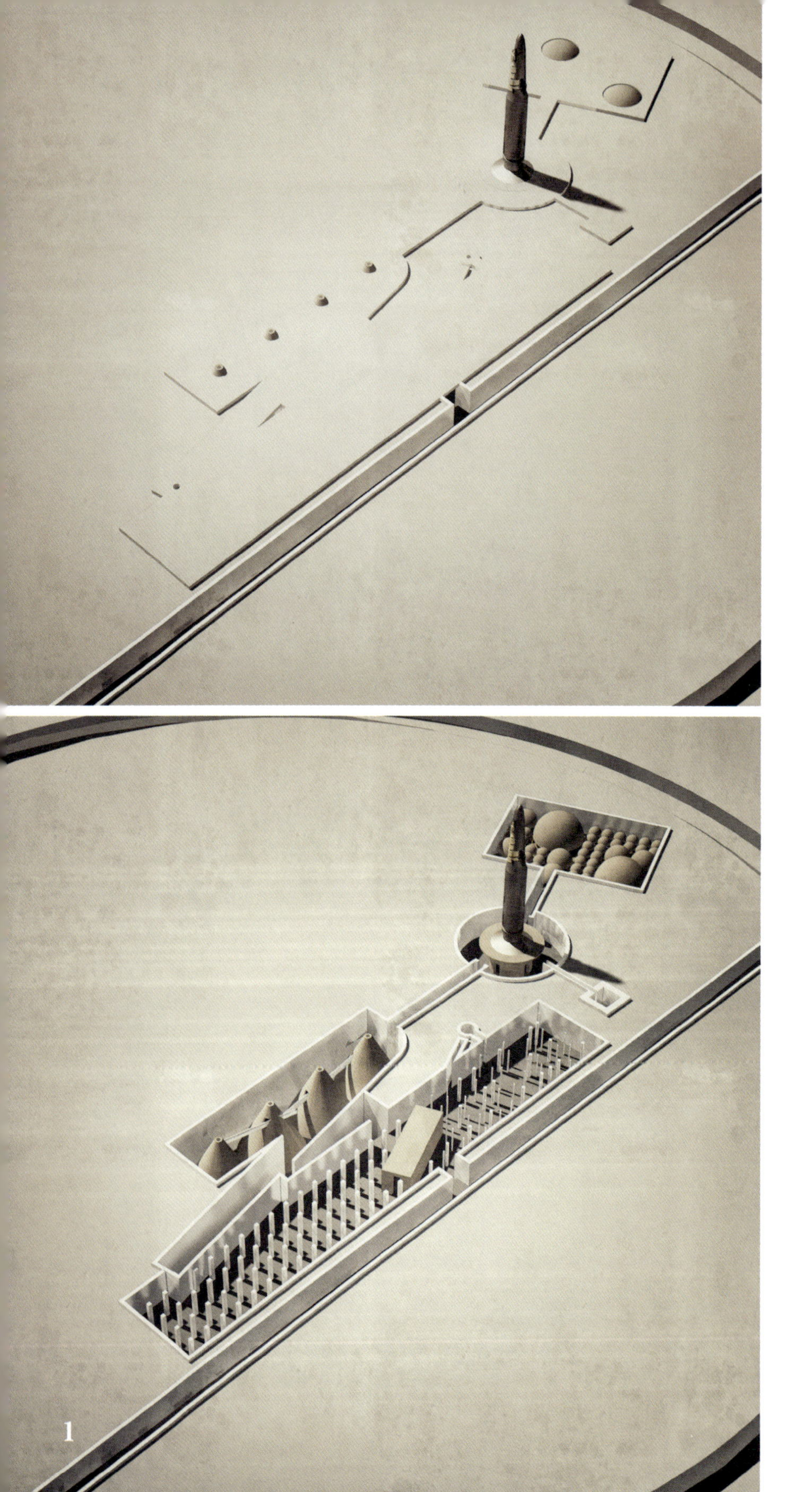

1

Revealing

Color, combined with material, is an amazing device for making architecture visible. When the Danish architect Asger Jorn moved to Albissola, he made the space of his Ligurian studio visible, revealing it to us by emphasizing the color and the material. His advice was followed in the Marseille Docks, where each space is characterized by color. Mind you, color does not exist by itself; it lives in the material that hosts it. In Marseille, the color is hosted and takes on life in the ceramics; each courtyard of the long building (350 meters enclosing four courtyards) is characterized by a color. The idea was to set up the courtyards as they had been decorated for the festivals of centuries past. One goes from courtyard to courtyard, from color to color, from space to space.

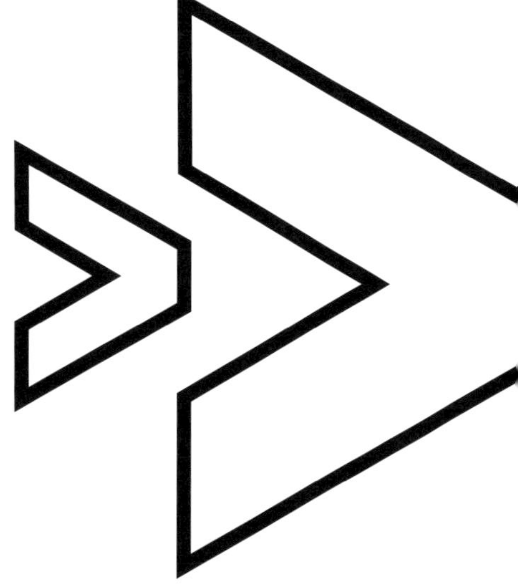

1. Jorn House Museum, detail
   of the flooring, 1957–73,
   Albissola Marina (Savona)

2. Restoration of the Marseille
   Docks, 2009–15

Revealing

Making architecture visible also passes through the object's iconicity. Making architecture at least in part similar to an icon makes it easily recognizable and memorable. In his works, Giuseppe Capogrossi used ideograms that were always similar to themselves; he controlled the space of the canvas through them by playing on the ambiguity between differentiation and repetition. In the building for the Italian Space Agency, a series of pavilions control the space in the same way. The pavilions relate to each other, but all together they define a clear layout principal. They are similar to ideograms but they are architectural ideograms and, as such, they are not two-dimensional and imply different spatialities

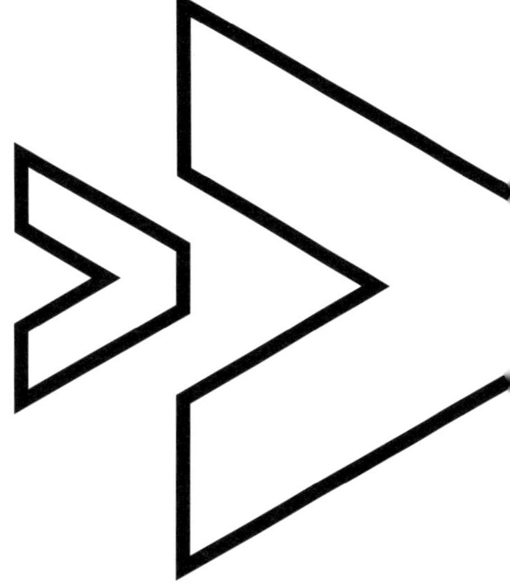

1. Giuseppe Capogrossi,
   Superficie 151 [Surface 151],
   detail, 1954

2. New A.S.I. (Italian Space
   Agency) headquarters,
   2012, Rome

Revealing

Hiding, covering—to reveal. Mantegna relies on a shroud to show Christ's absolute, desperate corporality, his becoming man through the tragedy of the Passion and his death. The shroud is the element that allows us to perceive this mystery and with it an apparent absence of hope. At the dawn of the twentieth century, Giacomo Boni discovered the Lapis Niger at the foot of the Arch of Septimius Severus. A few days later, the sacred area of the Lapis was uncovered. These finds showed the world that the Rome of Kings was not a mythical invention, as German historiographers had claimed, but a chiasmus of reality and mystery typical of Mediterranean civilizations. The project for covering, crossing, protecting, and visiting the sacred area of the Lapis Niger, the Rostra, and the Temple is the physical and evocative construction a shroud in ultra-high performance concrete (UHPC), made of material that is stretched and abandoned to its weight like a cloth. It reveals by concealing and evokes the mystery of a myth that becomes archeology.

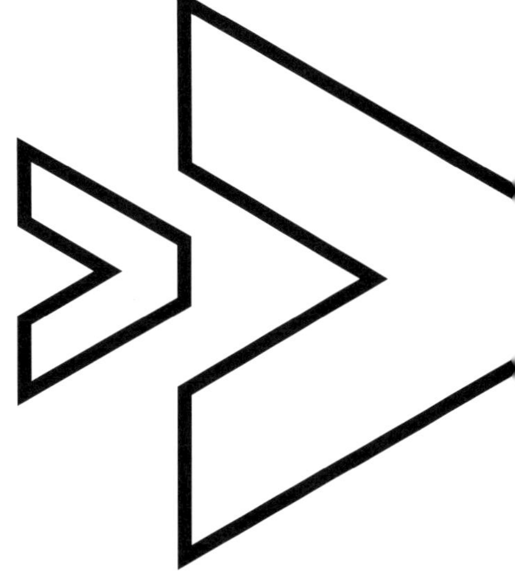

1. Andrea Mantegna, *The Lamentation of Christ*, 1470–74, Pinacoteca di Brera, Milan

2. Project for the Lapis Niger Area, 2024, Colosseum Archaeological Park, Roman Forum, Rome

Revealing

In the background of Giorgione's *The Tempest* there is a building of utter modernity. It rises up out of the walls like a tower that drops down toward the river below. Its masonry is absolutely simple, completely anonymous but adjectivized by three sculptural elements: the large arched opening, the balcony that runs the full width of the facade, and a stunning slanted roof canopy that overhangs the facade. The building painted by Giorgione reveals a compositional approach in which a simple, naturally anonymous, though well-composed building is characterized by a few precise elements in relation to each other. These elements have the capacity to reveal the architecture to us.

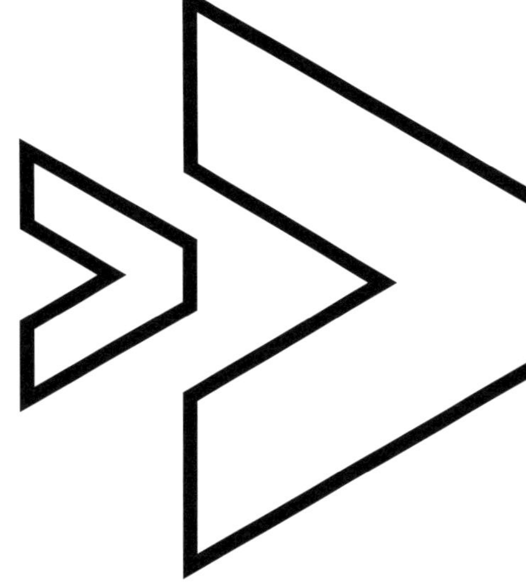

1. Giorgione, *The Tempest*,
   1506–08, Gallerie
   dell'Accademia, Venice

2. Nautical Institute of
   Gallipoli, 2020

1

Revealing

The interiors of public spaces must not be silent; they have to have the courage to make themselves visible though what we like to call their narrative. This leads to thinking about an architecture whose interiors as well—not unlike theatrical drama— reveal the elements of which it is formed. These are interiors in which the slabs, the pillars, the openings, the ramps, and so forth can define the scene of an event in which one would like to participate. It is a set, however, that can remain the background, that does not get in the way the actors' performance. This can only be achieved by undermining the modernist dialectic between figure and background: the background must also become the figure and the figure the background as well. There are no preconceived rules for breaking down the dualism between the figure and the background. To go beyond dualism, one has to rely intuitively on that taste that, if used well, makes it possible to understand the limit beyond which sound intentions backfire.

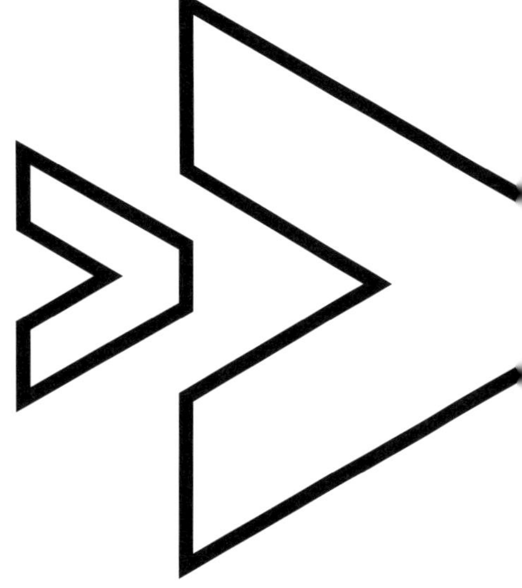

1. Mario Sironi, *Composition*,
   1958

2. Project for the Biblioteca
   di Lettere, Università
   La Sapienza, 2022, Rome

Revealing

The body is a body insofar as it reveals itself; without making itself visible, the body does not exist, it vanishes into nothingness. The body is made up of limbs; their position allows us to infer whether it is still or in motion. Art, photography, and architecture are allowed to stage a specific moment in the life of bodies. Piero della Francesca's angels open the curtain of the Virgin's apparition. Their gesture is courtly but not emphatic, we intuit their body but we also understand it is an angelic, almost intangible body. In Giovanni Michelucci's Church of the Autostrada, the "limbs" of the architectural body are represented in their effort to sustain the building, better still in the moment in which their effort has come to fruition. Unlike Piero della Francesca's limbs, Michelucci's are completely terrestrial, they are completely tangible. Piero della Francesca's and Michelangelo's bodies define the poles on which Italian figurative corporeality has been established. As far as architecture is concerned, we can put Terragni and Michelucci at these two poles.

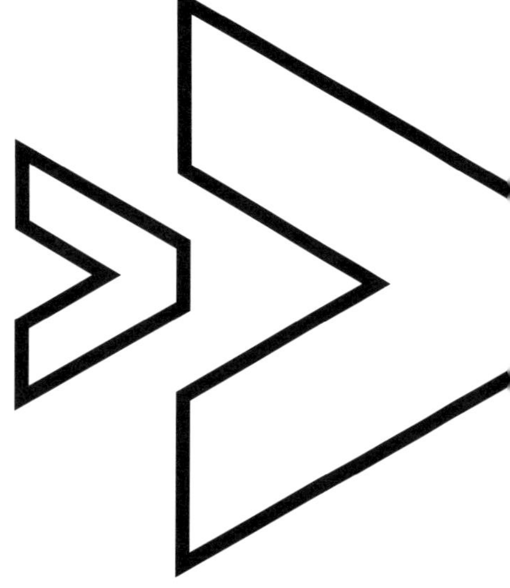

1. Piero della Francesca, *Madonna del Parto*, detail, 1455–65, Monterchi (Arezzo)

2. Giovanni Michelucci, church of San Giovanni Battista ("Church of the Autostrada"), 1960–64, Florence

1

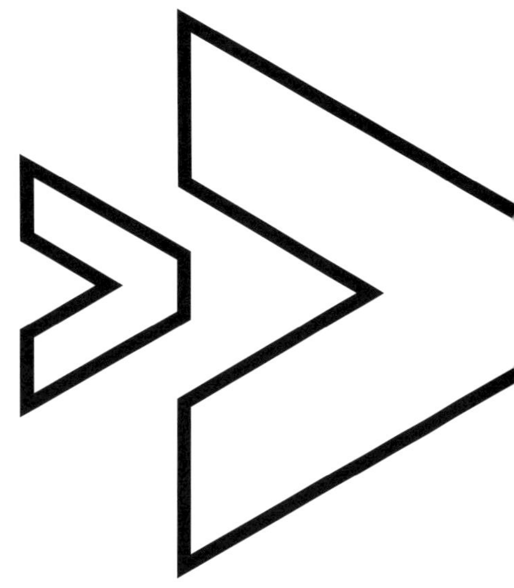

e•voke /i vōk'/ v.t. (L *ēvocāre* = e- E- + vocāre "to call").
– 1. to call up or produce (memories, feelings, etc.). 2.
to elicit or draw forth: "His comment evoked many pro-
tests. 3. to produce or suggest through artistry and
imagination: "a poem that evokes sounds and images or
uban life. 4. to call up; cause to appear' summon: to
evoke a spirit from the dead.

From *Random House Webster's College Dictionary*

Without evoking, without alluding to something other than itself, architecture is demeaned then dies. In the photograph by Ugo Mulas, Lucio Fontana is caught at the moment in which he is cutting the canvas vertically, an act that showed the will to go beyond representation. In his diaries Paul Klee kept repeating that the task of art is to unveil the invisible. Klee did not mean anything mystical or transcendent by this, he simply sought to evoke an expressive dimension that was suspended, verisimilar, real and unreal at the same time. In this dimension, common to Klee, Fontana, Burri, and others, things take on a certain mystery that continually questions us without ever fully conceding itself. Architecture has the potential, the ability to evoke this verisimilar dimension suspended between the real and the unreal, between the tangible and the intangible. When this happens there is a veritable apparition: an evocative apparition. To be such, architecture always has to refer to a sequence of other works of architecture, art, film, or anything else that activates what can be called evocative potential. Looking closely, evocative architecture actually lives through its genealogy. But this is not enough; there is in fact another evocation that goes beyond the figurative, the one that is spatial. The evocative potential of space refers not only to sight but to the other senses as well. In Borromini's Church of San Carlo alle Quattro Fontane, we enter a space, a body of walls that envelops us. As it does, this space, like that of Giovanni Michelucci's Church of the Autostrada or Giancarlo De Carlo's School of Education in Urbino, triggers primordial sensations that are awakened through the architecture we are experiencing. Architecture's evocative potential is generated by both its exterior image and by the interior space; one is indispensable to the other. If the image were to win out over the space, we would have more or less kitsch icons; if the space were to prevail, we would have informal architecture that, as such, is incapable of rooting its presence in us. Here too, the proposed hypothesis is that of an a-dual, syncretic, inclusive architecture that balances the evocative potential of the image with that of the space. Image and space have to evoke together, they have to make themselves indispensable to one another.

A caveat is needed here. Evoke is a transitive verb: one evokes something more or less precise sharing it with others. Of late, there seems to be a trend toward architecture that attempts to eliminate evocative potential. We speak of "non-referential architecture" that eliminates the referent and in doing so evokes itself alone. The forms of this architecture are iconic, simple, even banal; they do not communicate deliberately; they are laconic and elusive, at most they can express well-meaning, generic ecological or social sentiments. This is architecture that reduces evocative potential to mere communication and does so by shortening the narrative, almost making it superfluous. We want to think about a different kind of architecture, an architecture that, citing Lucio Fontana, cuts through the canvas of non-referentiality; an architecture that expresses bodily, visual, and tactile sensations and memories, even at the cost of getting its hands dirty by bringing itself into play.

voking

The evocative value of architecture must not be forsaken, lest it tumble into oblivion. In ancient times, the Tiber Island in Rome was like a ship, complete with bulkhead and prow. If one intends to express a shared language that can be predisposed to becoming part of a common expressiveness, one has to pass through evocation. This is a difficult step: if the evocation is too literal, it lapses into citation and, consequently, into kitsch. The cord that holds together the images and the words that name them has to be loosened, being wary not to lapse into the didascalic. A dose of abstraction helps. The abstract or at least stylized form communicates, but it does not yield itself completely. A building can recall something, but it cannot conform with what it recalls. It can also recall several things at once, but it must be very careful to maintain the synthesis and, with it, the unity of its overall form.

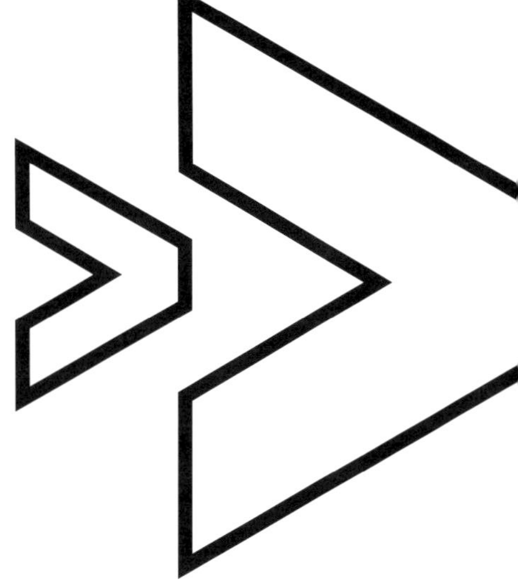

1. Relief of primitive obsidian stones

2. Project for "The Stone," a residential building, 2022, Cervinia

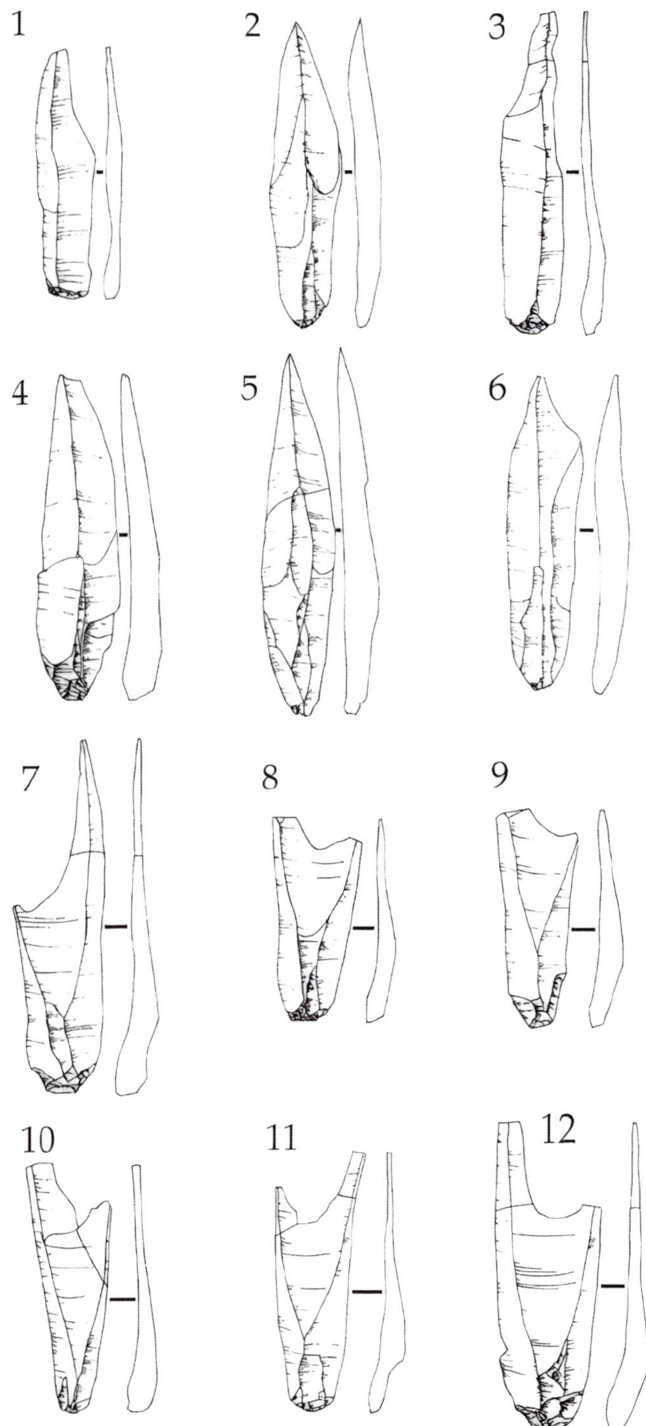

1
2
3
4
5
6
7
8
9
10
11
12

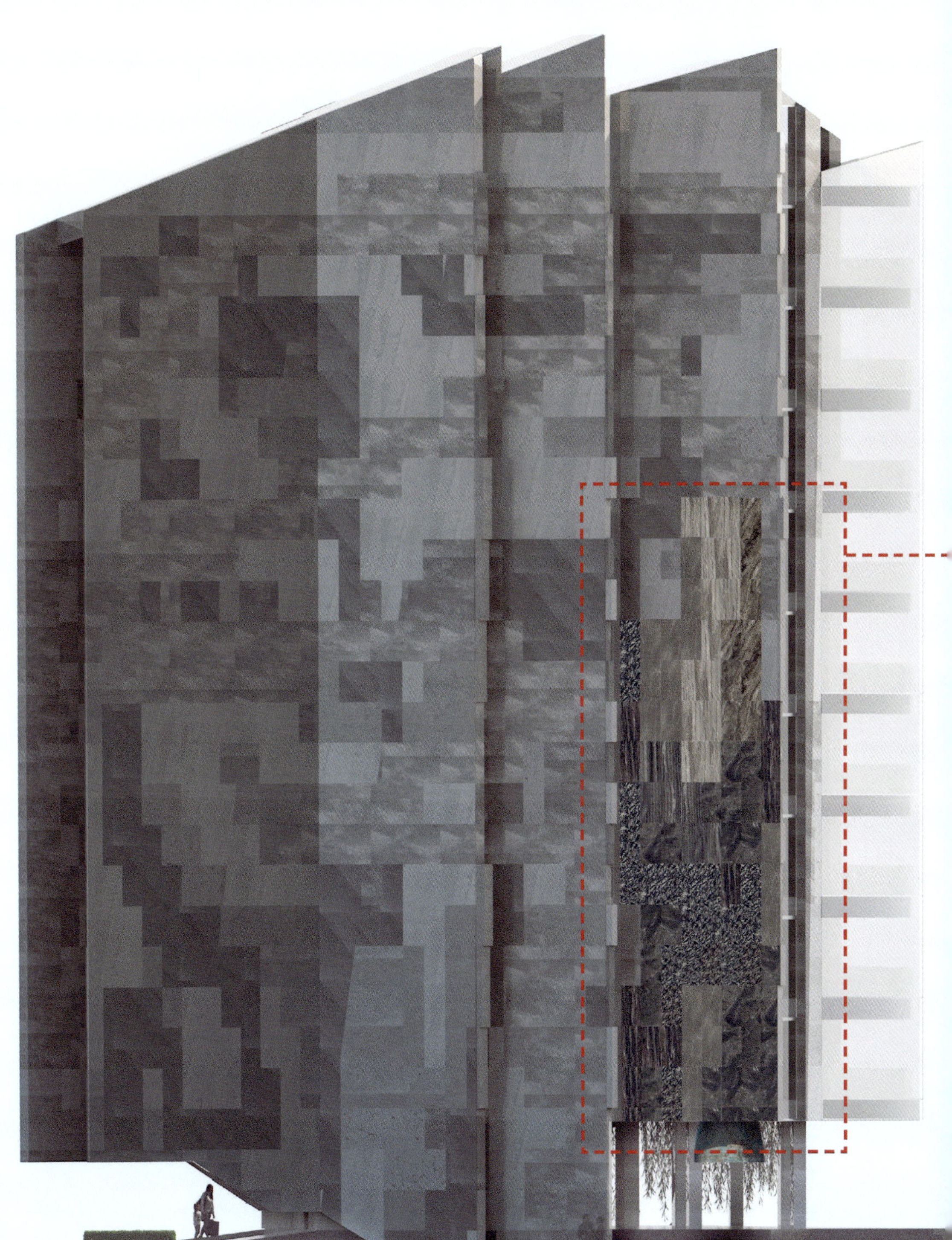

voking
In the 1950s, Pier Luigi Nervi conceived of particular, highly sculptural pillars. They start on a cross plan and end in a rectangle so that the shaft describes a complex ribbed surface that, by analogy, may recall the twisted columns of the medieval Basilica of Saint Peter. The plasticity of Nervi's pillars is not design, it not extraordinary for the sake of being extraordinary. The pillars evoke ancestral bodies, pre-human idols like the Cyclopes, that, as in the Palazzo del Lavoro in Turin, support the sky of the roofing. The project for the Science Museum in Rome evokes these idols whose presence has been delegated the task of configuring and protecting the public space below. In some Italian Romanesque churches, such as Saint Mary in Cosmedin in Rome, there is a body (that of church itself) that contains other bodies (the cathedra, the ambo, the ciborium). Entering these churches, there is sense of representation that has gone on for centuries and continues to welcome us.

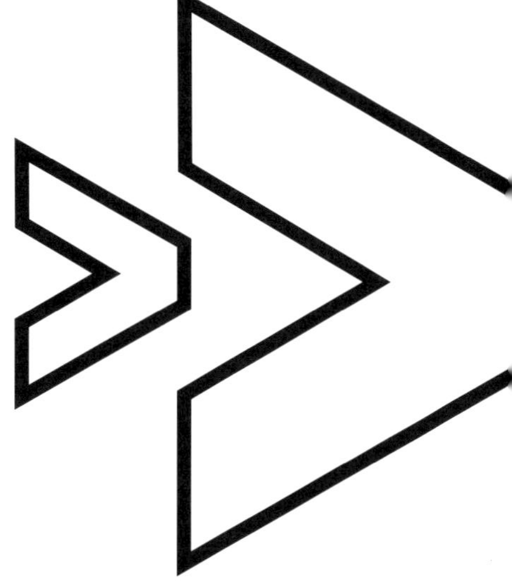

1. Pier Luigi Nervi, pillar of
   Palazzo del Lavoro, technical
   section, 1960, Turin

2. Project for the Science
   Museum in Rome, 2022

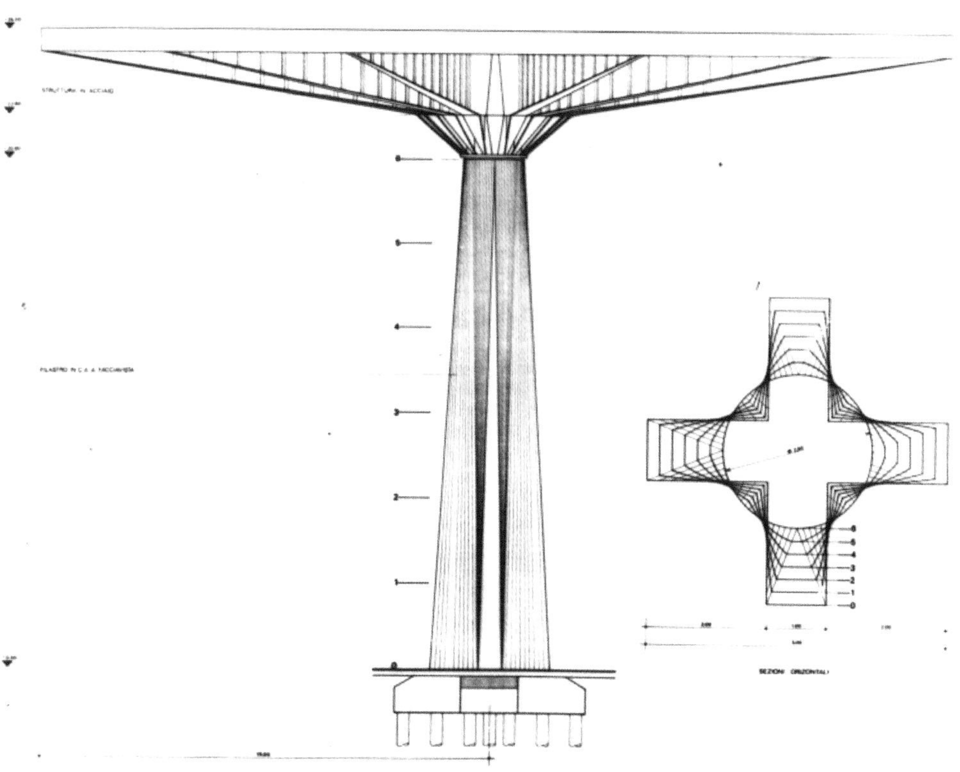

STRUTTURA IN ACCIAIO
PILASTRO IN C.A. NECCANISTA
SEZIONI ORIZZONTALI

voking
Italian architecture understood the extent to which
the icons of modernity, in their essentiality, could
become symbolic objects. This is an important lesson of Futurism and later of Italian Rationalism.
In the poster designed by Adalberto Libera for the
exhibition of the Movimento Italiano Architect-
tura Razionale of 1928, there is a solitary, hieratic, reinforced concrete pillar at the top of which
iron bars stick out with a certain heraldic flair.
An important detail: the pillar is not abstract; it
is a body that casts a shadow on which it actually
seems to stand. Libera's intention is clear: to evoke
the sense of a new figurativeness that was both
modern and ancestral, a presence that was "primordial," as people were then saying. In the project for the Ospedale degli Incurabili in Naples,
the large full-height interior space is the stage on
which the ramp and walkway—treated as primordial elements—act out a dialogue, the sense of
which is entirely subservient to the real protago-
nist appearing through them, the space that contains them.

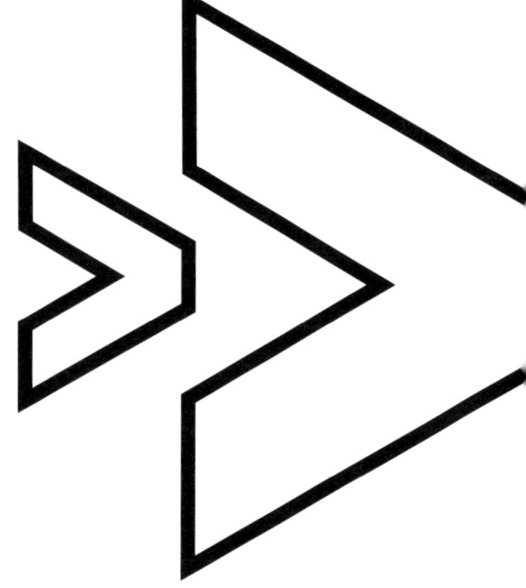

1. Pier Luigi Nervi, project
   for the "Palazzo dell'Acqua
   e della Luce E42," 1939

2. Project for the Ospedale
   degli Incurabili, 2020,
   Naples

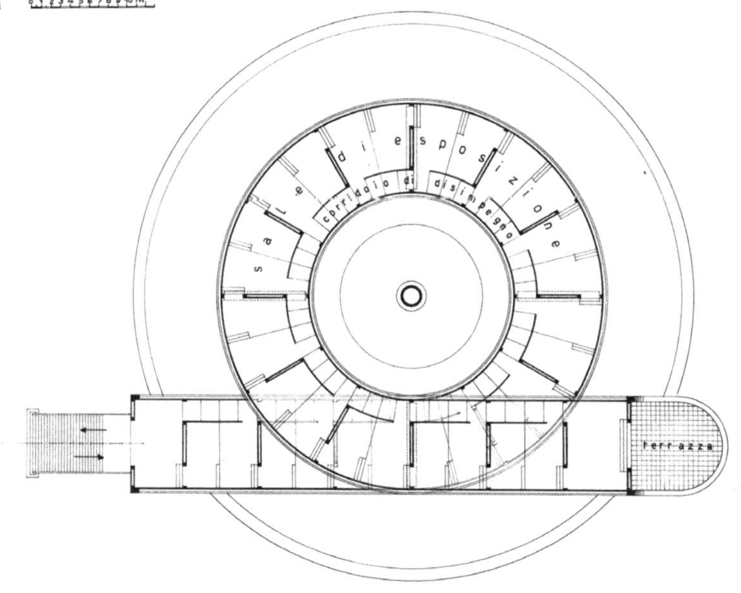

PROGETTO DEL PALAZZO DELL'ACQUA
E DELLA LUCE PER LA E.42.

Pianta 0 1 2 3 4 5 6 7 8 9 10 m.

STATUA IN MARMO DI
GEREMIA DA COSIMO
FANZAGO, CAPPELLA
DI SAN IGNAZIO DI
LOYOLA, FONDATORE
DELLA COMPAGNIA DI
GESÙ, GESÙ NUOVO,
SPACCANAPOLI,
NAPOLI, ITALIA

# voking

Architectural elements can be evocative and they can be so in two different ways. The first could be defined as literal. In it, pillars, beams, slabs, and whatnot, independently or in their interrelationships, allude to a body, or better said to an architectural body. In the second, it is as though these elements were fused together to give rise to a unified plasticity, so as to merge the individual architectural personalities together. This is the plasticity of the necks of Piero della Francesca's women; tumescent, pompous necks that still retain, and expose almost with pride, a cold sensual grace. It is this sculptural grace, firm and bit out of scale, still mindful of its rural origins, that the project for the Church of Olbia sought to evoke.

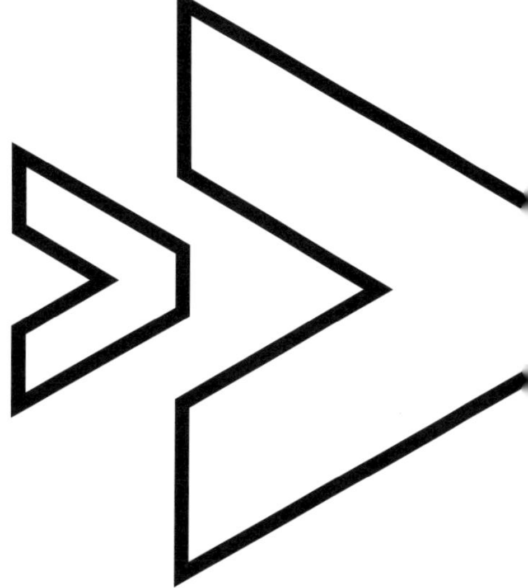

1. Piero della Francesca,
   The Dream of Constantine,
   from the *Legend of the
   True Cross*, Basilica of San
   Francesco, 1458–66, main
   chapel, Arezzo

2. Project for the new parish
   of Sant'Ignazio da Laconi,
   2021, Olbia

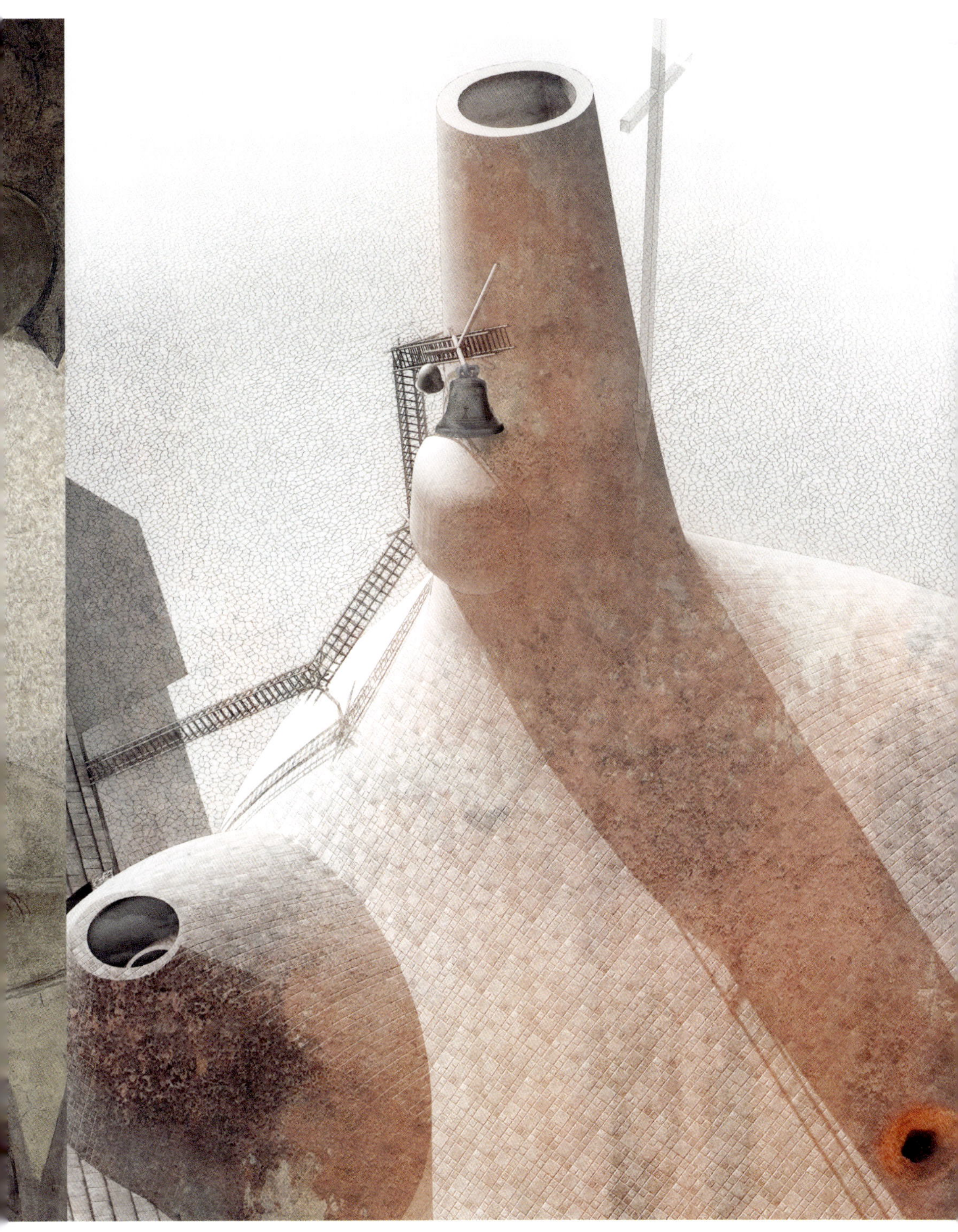

voking

L'immagine sospesa is the title of Paolo Fossati's fine book on Italian art and architecture of the 1930s. The theme of "the suspended image" is recurrent in Italy and has been interpreted across a broad spectrum that goes from metaphysical figuration to lyrical abstraction. Of particular interest are the hybridizations between what might appear to be two opposites. They recount of how, since Giotto's time, there has been an attempt in Italy to make the figure and abstract atmosphere coexist, as if the goal were the search for a dimension by now beyond dualisms. Perhaps it is this research for a non-dual form that is the peculiarity—the uniqueness—of great Italian art. The suspension of the image is undoubtedly evocative but, at the same time, exactly what it is evocative of is not clear. One might say that the suspended image evokes an enigma, in which case it is as though the forms, which are most often clear and well-defined, ask us something in an incomprehensible language for which we are missing more or less essential pieces of the code. Suspending the form, evoking a mystery or, if nothing more, an enigma so as to once again re-enchant what surrounds us, first and foremost architecture.

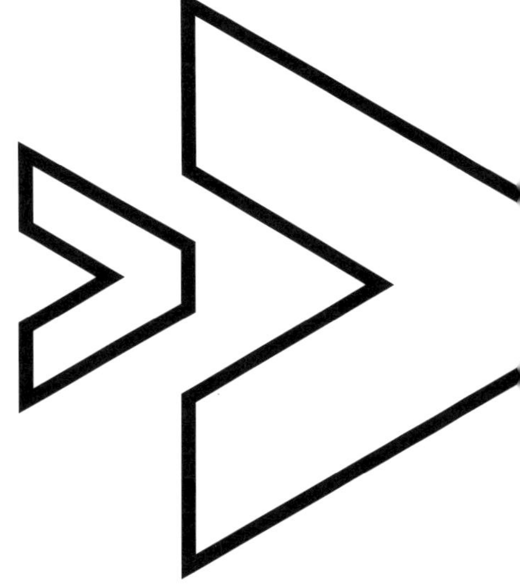

1. Luigi Ghirri, *Naples*, 1981

2. Horizontal Tower, 2008–14,
   Fiera Milan-Rho

voking

In the fresco of the Camera degli sposi in Mantua, Mantegna breaks through the ceiling with an opening to the sky. From the balustrade of that opening, joyful putti, animals, and angels gaze outward, making the illusion more tangible. Mantegna's gesture is clear, defined, even elemental. In the school in Zugliano, the building seems to open to the sky revealing the inner courtyard. An attempt was made here to emulate Mantegna's primary gesture by giving the building a more expansive spatiality. This allows the children to experience two spatialities: the enclosed one of classrooms and that of the common courtyard open to sky. Evoking different expressive dimensions through equally diverse spatialities, each in turn evocative of a shared way of being together. Spatialities in which what is spacious evokes what is smaller, light carries with it shadow, and hardness always remembers to come to terms with softness.

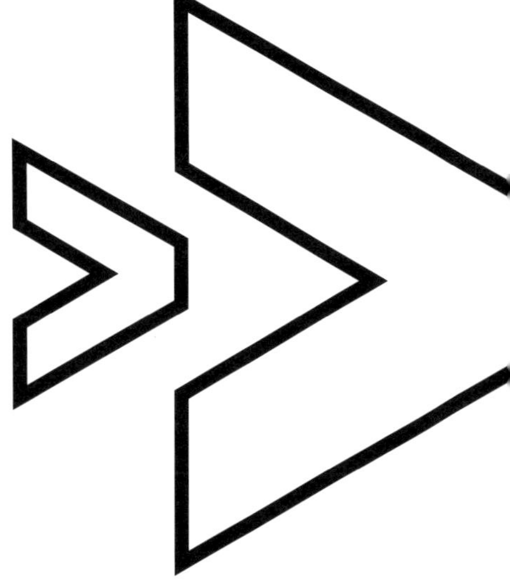

1. Andrea Mantegna, *Camera
   degli Sposi (Camera picta)*,
   detail, 1465–74, Ducal
   Palace, Mantua

2. Project for the new school
   complex in Centrale, 2015,
   Grumolo Pedemonte,
   Zugliano (Vicenza)

voking

A vintage photograph portrays the architect Luigi Moretti sitting in his studio posing: he looking out at us with piercing eyes, surrounded by his world. It is an inclusive world, not at all dual, in which a statue of a Madonna and Child coexists naturally with an abstract painting. Resting on the table in front of Moretti, there are three rolled drawings that seem to give the perspective for the shot. In designing the coverings for the Vado Ligure secondary school, memory probably went back, involuntarily, to these rolled drawings, to their primary, silent evocative power. This evocative power was amplified by covering the intrados of the vault with colorful, somewhat timeless images. The choice to represent this project with a ceramic model is not accidental. This material evokes the corporeal, the imperfect, and the unfinished; characteristics wc like to exalt in our work.

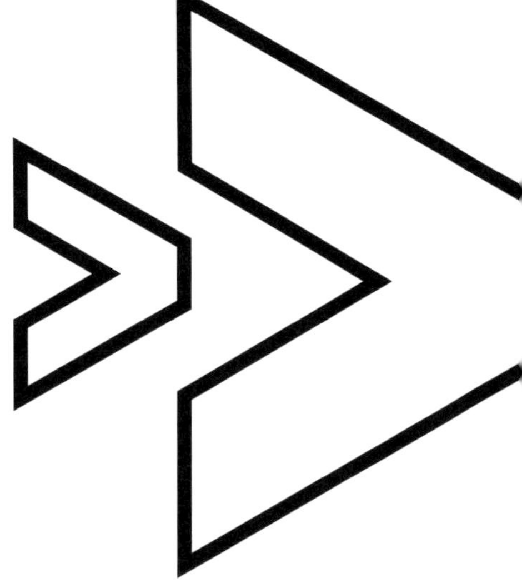

1. Project for the school
   complex in Vado Ligure
   (Savona), 2020

2. Portrait of Luigi Moretti in
   his studio in Rome, late-
   1950s

1

Evoking

In 1970 Maurizio Sacripanti presented an extraordinary project for the theater in Cagliari. In it, a grid envelops the theater's interior. At the ceiling, it houses an almost infinite series of skylights that descend dramatically into the hall. On the ground floor, instead, it extrudes into movable blocks that can be arranged according to the set's needs. The principle by which the grid extrudes to the sky and on the ground is the same, but the elements it configures (the skylights above and the seats on the ground) are different. In Sacripanti's project, the extreme morphological synthesis corresponds to the highest degree of spatial articulation. Sacripanti's concept was evoked in the mosque in Sokhna on the Red Sea and, sparingly, his forms as well. In the mosque, the roof slab is a frame that punctuates the arrangement of the skylights and the architectural elements; it holds them together in an architectural landscape that seeks to dialogue with the mighty desert mountains surrounding the building.

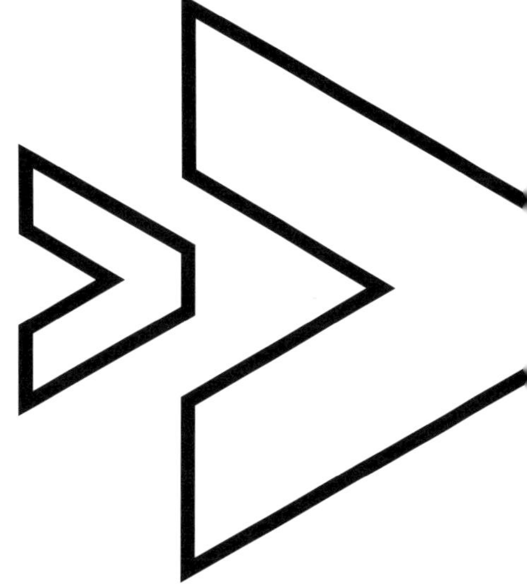

1. Maurizio Sacripanti,
   with F. Frigerio, A. Nonis,
   G. Pellegrineschi
   (automatisms),
   G. Perucchini (structures),
   F. Purini, A. Perilli, Project
   for the new Teatro Lirico
   di Cagliari, 1964–65

2. Mosque in Sokhna, 2019–
   in progress, Monte Galala,
   Egypt

voking

There is no need to represent the body; it can be evoked. Alberto Burri's painting might seem abstract, but it is not; if anything, it can be considered the highest degree of abstract sublimation granted to the body. Burri is corporeal; the texture, the grain, the more or less explicit roughness, the color mixed with the material and the shadow it casts define images that appear to be the details of bodies, almost alienating zooms of them. In the *Cretto* in Gibellina, we enter the wounds of one these bodies and, in walking along those winding streets of the town that was, we still hear the echo of the earthquake's drama. In Burri's silent, hieratic work, we also feel the genealogy of Italian painting from the Roman and Byzantine to the modern; we actually perceive its sublimation in form that cannot be anything but partially abstract. The ability to evoke is the whip with which Burri seems to tame abstraction.

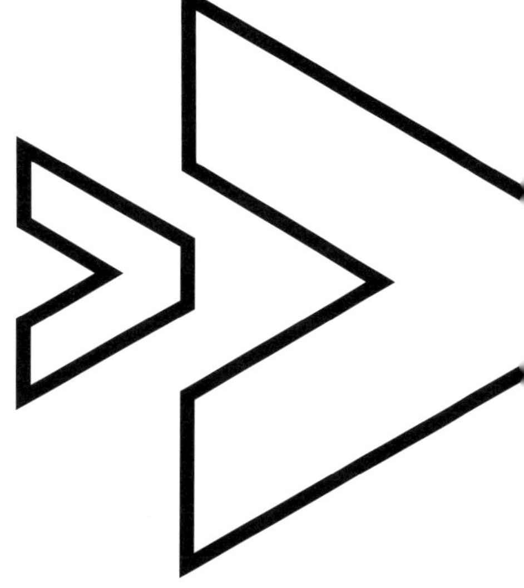

1. Alberto Burri, *Copertina*
   [Cover], 1953

2. Reuse of the ex-Caserma
   Ferdinando di Savoia–
   Ministero degli Interni,
   2015, Rome

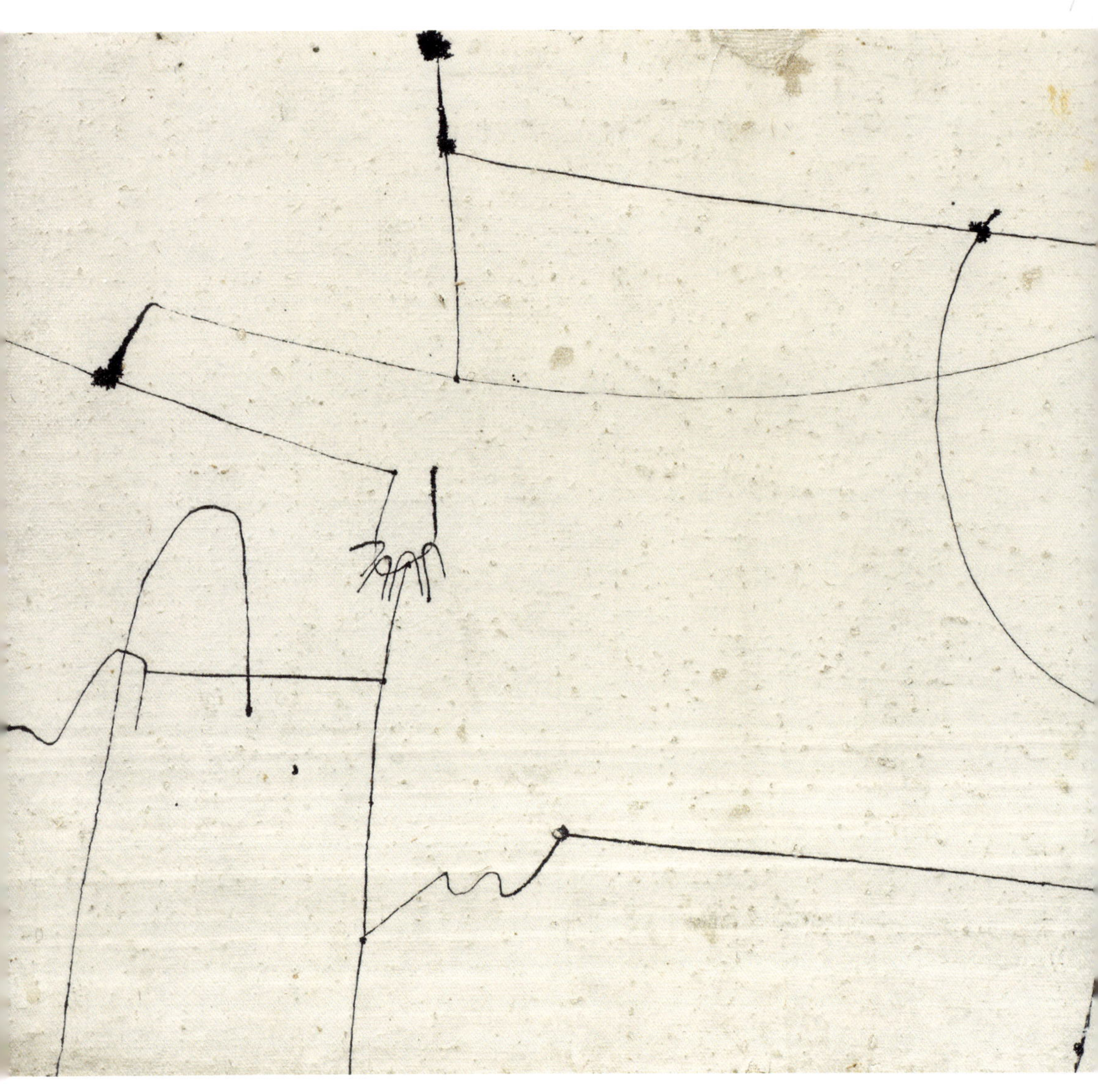

voking

Sculptural form is evocative by nature but, mind you, it is only so if it determines a space. Evoking is incomplete if it stops at the image, just as space is useless if it is not embodied in a figure. In 1967, Luigi Moretti proposed a completely heretical project for the sanctuary on the Sea of Galilee (Lake Tiberias), in which figure and space exalted each other to the point of paroxysm. The project, which owes a great deal to baroque fluorescence might seem excessive but this excess is not at all gratuitous. It can be explained by both representative and territorial reasons: representative in the sense that Moretti sought to reiterate the importance of the sacred event that had taken place there; territorial in that it is as if the sanctuary itself were a device to make the lake "evocative."

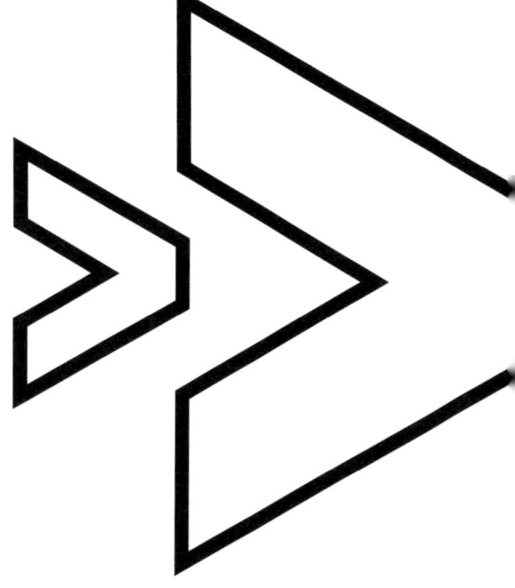

1. Luigi Moretti, project for
   the sanctuary on the Sea
   of Galilee (Lake Tiberias),
   1967, Tabgha, Palestine

2. International competition
   for a rest and service area,
   2018, Sarzamin, Iran

 voking

Modernity, paradoxically, was born in parallel with the attraction for ruins. The letter in which Raphael urged Pope Leo X to preserve the beauty of "dead" architecture can be considered the first deliberate testimony of a new sensibility. Romanticism would later base its aesthetics on ruins, to the point of actually "ruining" some buildings constructed from scratch. The ruin has the capacity to evoke something else today; it has become the representation of the dissent against the seemingly polished, perfect technological world of design architecture. This world tends toward the immaterial, toward the elimination of the body, while the ruin reminds us of our corporeality and, with it, the wholly human need to see bodily physicality reflected in our surroundings.

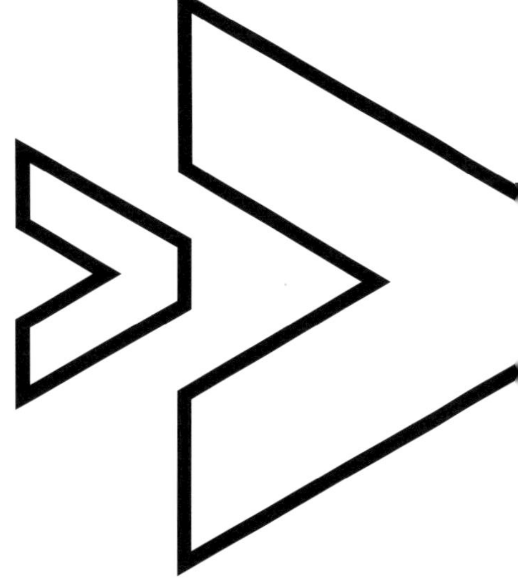

1. Temple E (of Hera or
   Aphrodite), fifth century BC,
   Selinunte Archaeological
   Park (Trapani)

2. Mosque in Sokhna, 2019,
   Monte Galala, Egypt

Evoking

The evocation of the forest and the clearing are two major themes in architecture: the hypostyle space that, like the Basilica Cistern in Istanbul, seems to open to infinity suddenly through the moonlight reflected on the water.

The IULM exhibition space is completely enclosed in exposed concrete, recalling the memory of the industrial world of Sironi's Milanese outskirts, inhabited by Scerbanenco's characters. We decided to insert a single circular opening in this space, a moon by Magritte, at the top left. When Fabrizio Plessi mounted the building's first show, he made his *Foresta Blu* dialogue with this moon, imagining a world inhabited by the sound of water and ancient progenitors.

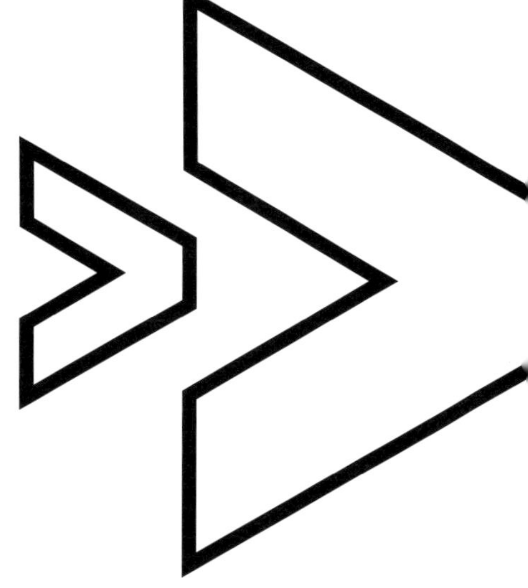

1. Basilica Cistern, 536 AD, Istanbul

2. Fabrizio Plessi, *Foresta Blu* [Blue Forest], 2014, IULM Exhibition Hall

voking
Ernesta Caviola's work on architecture is photographic work by a designer. The act of seeing is designing. The *punctum* of the Istanbul Cistern is the hypostyle mirrored in the water through the Roman faces and capitals, inverted, disfigured without torture, like parts of a stone Sisyphus that happily accepts the old and the new destiny of civic toil. Office cafeterias are often places with little spatial quality. The choice for the Italian Space Agency headquarters in Rome was to focus on an architectural monumentality, evocative of a celebratory space inside a collective place. Hypostyle, immersed in an artificial lake, the white almost classical columns are reflected on the slate floor. A series of variously colored skylights define an irregular language with respect to them.

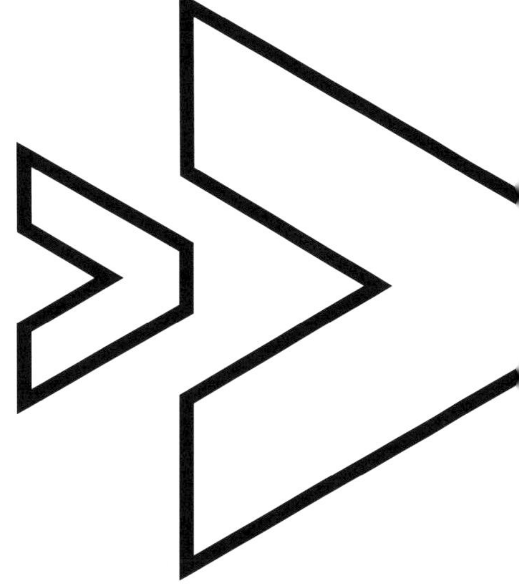

1. Basilica Cistern, 536 AD,
   Istanbul

2. New A.S.I. (Italian Space
   Agency) headquarters, 2012,
   Rome

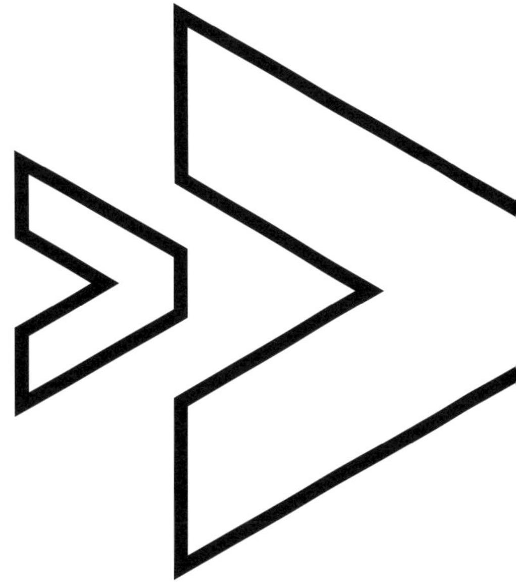

Transfiguring

trans•fig•ure /trans fig'yər/ v.t. [L *trānsfigūrāre*, "to change in shape," trans + figurare]. - 1. to change in outward form or appearance, transform. 2. to change so as to glorify or exalt.

From *Random House Webster's College Dictionary*

The Gospel of John recounts the myth of the Transfiguration. Christ takes some of the Apostles with him to Mount Tabor where he is transfigured, where he is changed in essence from a poor forsaken prophet to an astonishing divinity rising from the ground. The Apostles are terrified by the radical transformation of their prophet. Realizing this terror, Christ is transfigured again and comes back to being the human prophet they knew so well. Transfiguration, therefore, has to do with bodies; it also has a great deal to do with metamorphosis, but while the latter is irreversible, transfiguration is not. In Italian painting of the late Middle Ages and early Renaissance, bodies are transfigured. In the works of Beato Angelico these bodies live in two dimensions at once: the carnal and the spiritual. They are like resurrected bodies, which Christian doctrine does after all foresee. We can trace a possible genealogy of the transfigured form from Beato Angelico to contemporary art. In it one feels two opposing aspirations that merge into a chiasmus: the body's aspiration to transcendence and vice versa. Giuseppe Terragni's Casa del Fascio lives in the dimension of transfiguration. It is without doubt an architectural body; its windows are deep set and its frame is as clear and well-defined as the reference to which the work alludes, namely a generic Italian Renaissance palazzo. Through its abstraction, however, the corporeality of the Casa del Fascio is transfigured into another dimension. Here too, as in great Italian works, this dimension is a-dual. It actually lives between body and spirit without considering them irreconcilable. There is an evident distance between Terragni's Casa del Fascio and the architecture painted by Giotto but, seen closely, both enact transfiguration: both draw their strength from the transfigured architectural form. In the Church of the Autostrada, Giovanni Michelucci transfigures the primary figures such as the tent, the tree, the ruin, the clearing, and the staircase. We catch these references out of the corner of our eye, fleetingly, almost unconsciously, surely intuitively. We make them our own in a child-like way without going through the intellect, hence their strength. One of architecture's most important transfigurations is that of the architectural elements themselves. If transfigured, pillars, beams, slabs, and so forth can take on a value that transcends them, as great Italian painting teaches us. This can only happen if we consider these elements according to their own nature, as primordial if not archetypal elements. Considered in this sense, they are predisposed to being transfigured into something that is different from the model but still recalls it. The magic of Casa Malaparte in Capri lies in its ability to transfigure the primordial and subsequently anonymous architectural elements into an extraordinary object.

Transfiguring

Roberto Longhi posited a relationship between Dante and Masaccio, both of whom rendered the body as if torn between the human and the divine. The teachings of Italian medieval and early Renaissance art tell us that this dimension is not only figurative; it is spiritual as well. The body casts a shadow, and the shadow of Saint Peter is miraculous, it heals the lame. The septa of the Hall of Victory cast a shadow, a rhythmic shadow that leads our gaze to Lucio Fontana's sculpture at the back. The body, how it translates into architecture, is the expressive dimension of interest. It is a variable dimension that goes from raw carnality to transfigured carnality at the threshold of abstraction, like that of Persico, Nizzoli, and Fontana's Hall of Victory. Duality is abolished there: the body of the figurative statue in the back is balanced by the abstraction of the space in which it is placed. The statue and the space are indispensible to one another. Isolating them would be a crime.

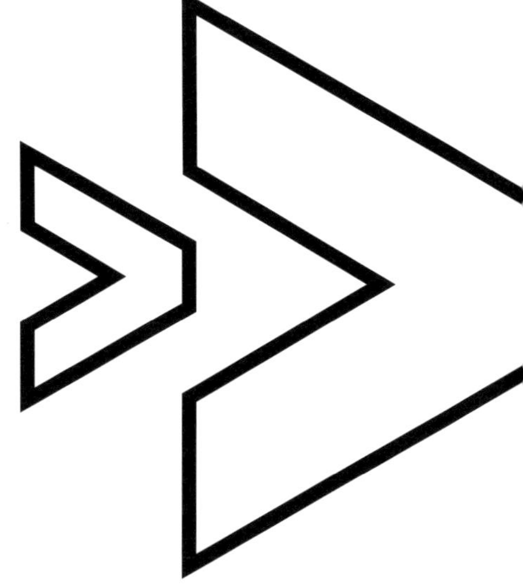

1. Masaccio, *Saint Peter Healing the Sick with His Shadow*, 1425–27, Brancacci Chapel, church of Santa Maria del Carmine, Florence

2. Marcello Nizzoli, Giancarlo Palanti, Edoardo Persico, Hall of Victory, 1936, Triennale di Milano. Sculptural group by Lucio Fontana

1

IL POPOLO ITALIANO HA
CREATO COL SUO SANGUE
L'IMPERO, LO FECONDERÀ
COL SUO LAVORO E LO DIFEN
DERÀ CONTRO CHIUNQUE
CON LE ARMI. MUSSOLINI
VI
1936 - A. XIV
TRIENNALE
DI MILANO
O S. A. CRIMELLA - MILANO (VI-5)

Transfiguring

Tullio di Albisola sought passionate, lyrical poetry. Lyricism can be considered a form of transfiguration, probably the most sophisticated one. An architectural etymon (a pillar, a beam, a slab) is a potential presence, amenable to evoking something that transcends its own appearance. It is as if the space were then populated by these figures that appear through two devices essential for transfiguration: light and color. There is a fundamental caveat in the transfiguration of architectural elements: they must not become objects of design, they must not undermine their semblance and, with it, what can be called their primordial, if not archetypal, origin. Transfiguration can only occur if the primordial origin of the architectural elements is respected. Christ is transfigured on Mount Tabor but, afterwards, he returns to being the humble preacher the Apostles know.

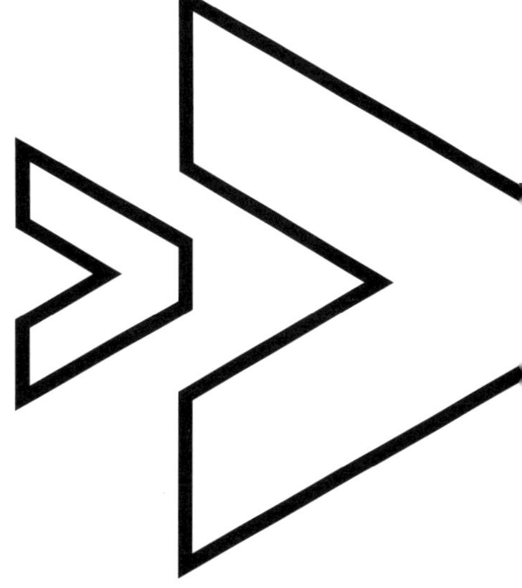

1. Tullio D'Albisola, *Anguria Lirica* [The Lyrical Watermelon], 1934, cover by Bruno Munari, Edizioni Futuriste "Poesia," Rome

2. New A.S.I. (Italian Space Agency) headquarters, 2012, Rome

POETI FUTURISTI

TULLIO D'ALBISOLA

L'ANGURIA LIRICA
(LUNGO POEMA PASSIONALE)

PRESENTAZIONE DI MARINETTI
(DELL'ACCADEMIA D'ITALIA)
CHIARIMENTO DI V. ORAZI

ILLUSTRAZIONI DI
BRUNO MUNARI

EDIZIONI FUTURISTE DI POESIA
PIAZZA ADRIANA 30 - ROMA

LITO - LATTA - SAVONA
LIRE CINQUANTA

Transfiguring

Places need to be transfigured: they appear in the moment in which they are transfigured. In the transfiguration, belonging and not belonging to the place merge together in a chiasmus. Going down from Capodimonte to the working-class neighborhood of Sanità in Naples, the houses seem to be fused with the outcrops on which they somewhat crookedly rise: the hardness of outcrops is made more evident by the battered houses often perched on them. In the design for the Ospedale degli Incurabili in Naples we sought a form of transfiguration: the outcrop became a wall that opens like a comb toward the top. The wall tongues rise toward the sky: they are part of the wall but they are also different from it. If we imagine cutting off these tongues, seeing them without the wall that engendered them, we would not be in Naples but in the placeless place of the most indulgent modernity. If, vice versa, we eliminated the tongues and kept the simple wall that engendered them, we would have the Naples of a worn-out cliché.

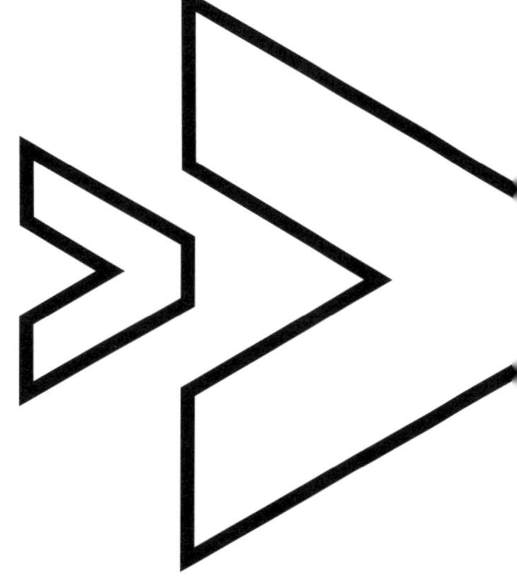

1. Temple of Mercury,
   Baiae Archeological Park,
   50 BC–140 AD

2. Project for the Ospedale
   degli Incurabili, 2020,
   Naples

Transfiguring

Mies van der Rohe kept repeating that architecture has nothing to do with the invention of forms. Apodictic like all of Mies' statements, this claim seems incomplete. Let's try to finish it: [...] has nothing to do with invention of forms, but it has a great deal to do with their transfiguration. The most important transfiguration is the one that makes the ordinary object extraordinary and does so by not distorting its appearance (therein the magic of transfiguration). Although the architecture in Giotto's paintings "does not invent forms," it is transported in another dimension that is at once fairytale-like and spiritual. It is noteworthy that instead of transforming the buildings' overall form, Giotto transfigures the individual architectural elements that compose them. In his representations, the pillars are elongated and become slender supports, the roofs taper to slabs, and the aediculae are stylized into utterly elemental forms; one even finds the cantilevers modern architects would employ centuries later. Composed together, the transfigured elements give rise to architecture in which the ordinary lives in a dimension that is neither real nor unreal; it is verisimilar.

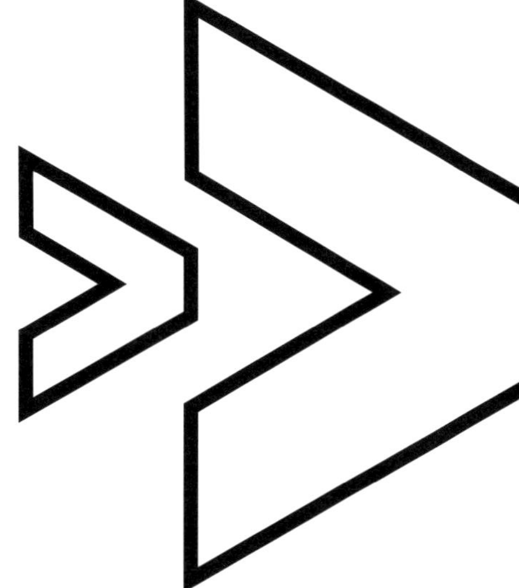

1. Project for the Scuola
   L. Ghiberti, 2022, Pelago
   (Florence)

2. Giotto, *Stories of Saint
   Francis*, detail, 1292–96,
   upper church, Assisi

Architecture is inherently stable; common sense teaches us that it is its duty to be stable. Futurism challenged this assumption of stability, and it did so by transfiguring what is stabile into something dynamic. Yet the transfiguration the Futurists proposed was not definitive; it did not actually allow dynamism to take over. Umberto Boccioni clarifies this in his *States of Mind*; the dynamism of *Those Who Go* needs the static nature of *Those Who Stay*, every state of mind needs its opposite in order to exist. Fixing dynamism means capturing it at a moment in which the memory of what came before still lingers, the moment when the motion had not yet been imprinted. In the facade of the BNL headquarters in Rome, we staged this frozen futurist dynamism, we tried to stage a motion—even a sparkling one—that no longer has any intention of moving. A transfigured motion that has found its expressive stillness.

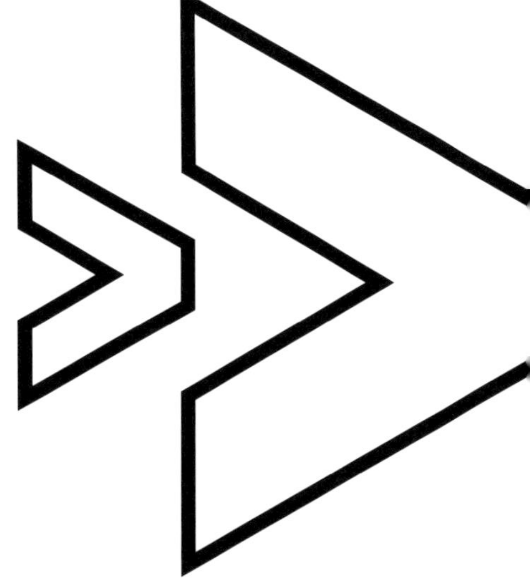

1. Giacomo Balla, *Velocità
   d'automobile* [Speeding
   automobile], detail, 1913

2. New BNL Paribas
   headquarters, 2016, Rome

1

Transfiguring

Luigi Moretti inserted the cast of a man's leg on the jamb of the side window of Casa del Girasole. Legend has it that it was Moretti's own leg, the one he had broken skiing, and that the sculpture had been made from a cast of his own plaster cast. Moretti's gesture is significant. In the Casa del Girasole he staged the tendentially abstract steps of modern architecture's transfiguration in architecture of the body. Moretti starts with the completely neoplastic wall he hangs on the main façade then treats the foundation as a stylized ruin and the inner courtyard as an ancestral cave. The cladding, in contrast, goes from the roughness of the bush-hammered slabs to the abstraction of polished travertine slabs. The transfiguration of the abstract into the corporeal ends with the leg itself. The Foro Italico in Rome is full of statues of sinewy athletes in pose. In the project for the tennis stadium, we tried to provide a set for these bodies, giving them a necessary architectural backdrop.

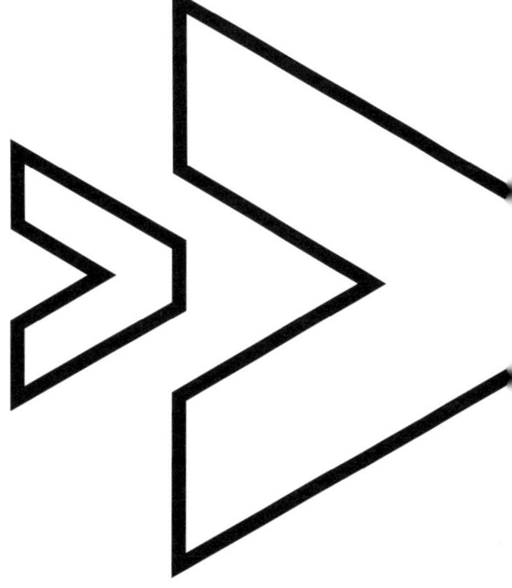

1. Luigi Moretti, "Il Girasole,"
   detail, side facade, 1947–50,
   Rome

2. Project for the main field of
   the Foro Italico, 2022, Rome

Transfiguring

In Valerio Zurlini's 1972 film *Indian Summer*, Alain Delon plays the role of an apathetic, world-weary high school teacher. At one point in the film, he runs off with one of his students, taking her to the cemetery in Monterchi where Piero della Francesca's *Madonna del Parto* was then conserved. The young teacher, who up until then had been rather blasé and had shown an almost aggressive indifference to the world, is transfigured. With unusual transport, he begins to speak about Piero della Francesca's magical beauty, about the enchantment of a painting that connects the celestial and the earthly with enigmatic precision. On hearing this unexpected discourse, the stunned young woman is also transfigured and, abandoning her bewilderment, she too becomes impassioned. What comes to mind is architecture that can transfigure our sensations and, with them, our feelings, without the vulgar use of the extraordinary and the exceptional.

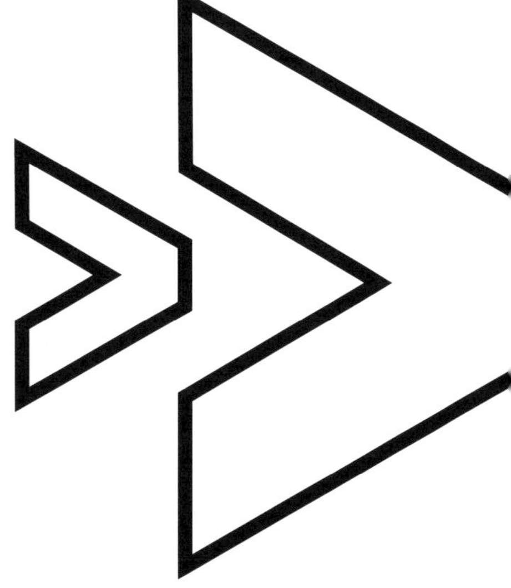

1. Piero della Francesca,
   Madonna del Parto, detail,
   1455–65, Monterchi
   (Arezzo)

2. Project for the new school
   complex in Centrale, 2015,
   Grumolo Pedemonte,
   Zugliano (Vicenza)

Transfiguring

In 1966 Pino Pascali mounted his vision of a sea in a room at L'Attico gallery in Rome. On the ground, a cloth meant to represent the sea was stretched over a structure in such a way as to create a series of sequenced "waves." From the wall, instead, the tail fins of what appeared to be a dolphin and an orca emerged. The "sea" was then struck by a twisted rod representing a lightning bolt. Pascali transfigured the composition's three elements (sea, fish, lightning) through a joyful language that was at once cheeky and lyrical. His installation demonstrates how bodies can be transfigured into ideas of themselves and that, in doing so, figure and abstraction can coexist quite well, to the point of creating an accessible, sharable language. Pascali mounted these transfigured bodies in the body–room of the gallery. By analogy, what again comes to mind are the Romanesque churches in which other architectural bodies—the cathedra, the ambo, the ciborium—are housed in the body of the church itself, and how these elements are delegated the responsibility for narrating the space that houses them.

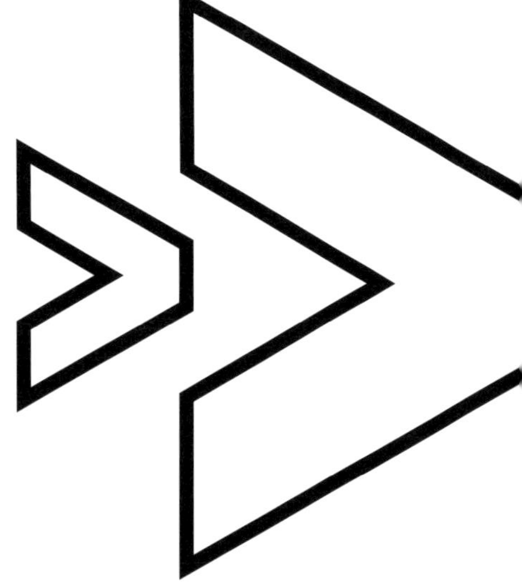

1. Ex Opificio D'Oria, Loano (Savona)

2. Pino Pascali, *The Sea*, installation at L'Attico gallery, October 29, 1966, Rome

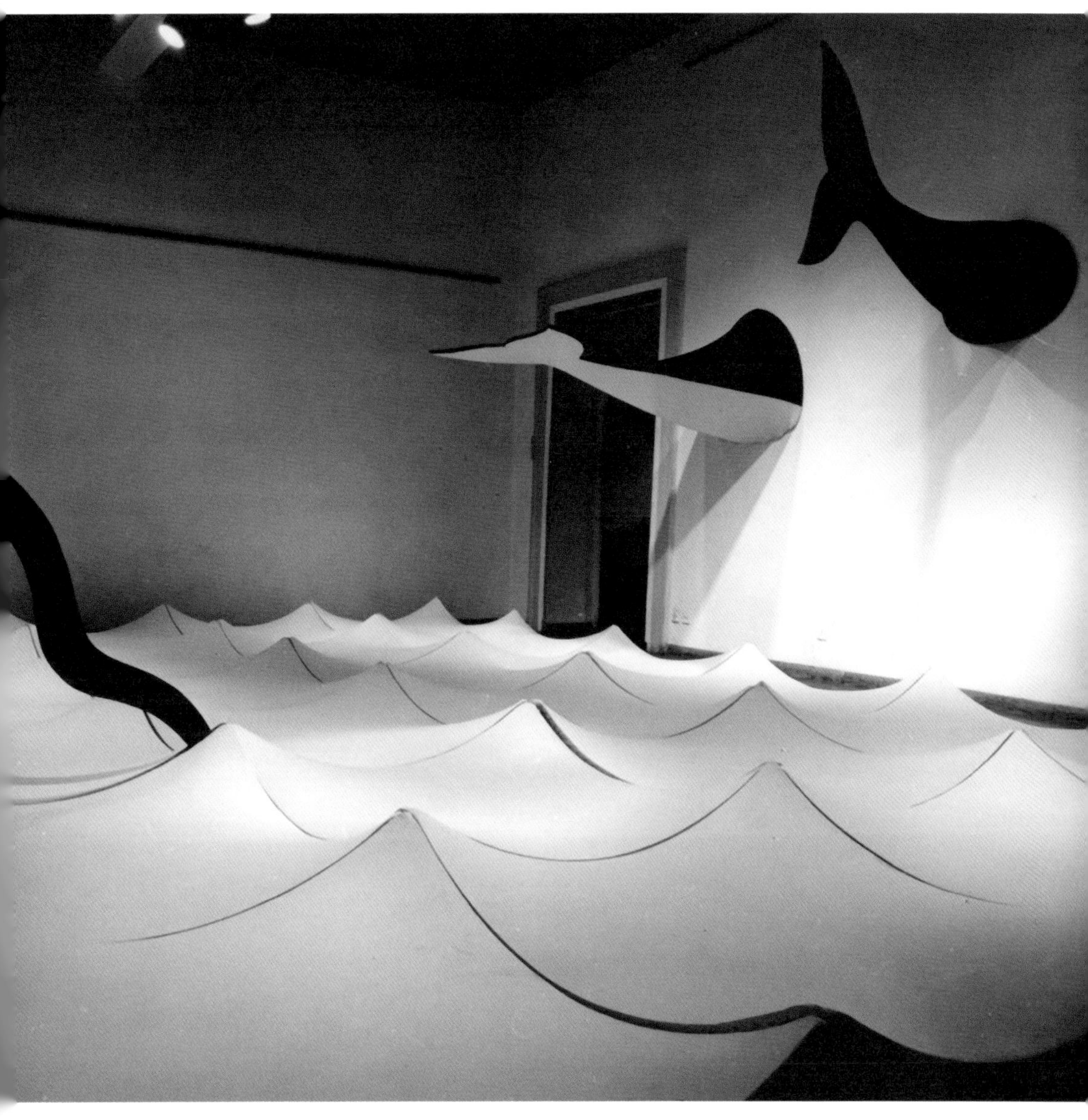

Transfiguring

The Vatican Pinacoteca conserves an exceptional painting by Beato Angelico depicting *Saint Francis Receiving the Stigmata*. Beato Angelico was a master in transfiguring land. In his paintings, terrains are modified, distorted, gain breadth or tend to be miniaturized. Angelico is even more radical in *Saint Francis Receiving the Stigmata*. There, the Holy Spirit is embodied in what appears to be a waterfall made of rocks that, bathed in light, reaches the Saint who opens his arms to the mountain cascade of divine light. In the project for the Monte Galala New Town in the Egyptian desert, we tried to transfigure the land, making it expressive; stylized by broken lines, we transposed it at the roofs of the houses.

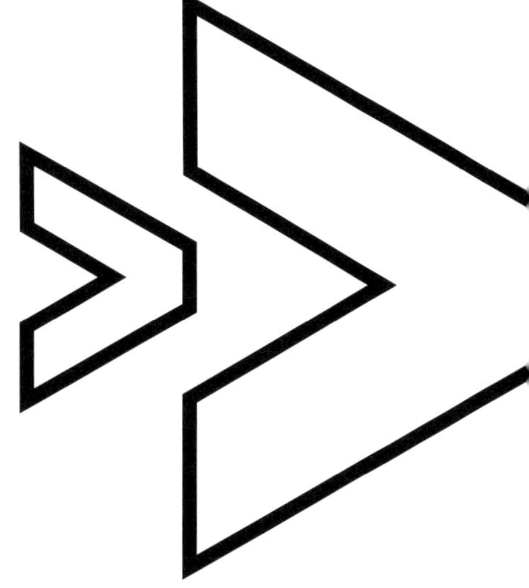

1. Monte Galala New Town,
   2018–under construction,
   Sokhna, Egypt

2. Beato Angelico, *Saint
   Francis Receiving the
   Stigmata*, 1440, The Vatican
   Museums, Pinacoteca, Rome

1

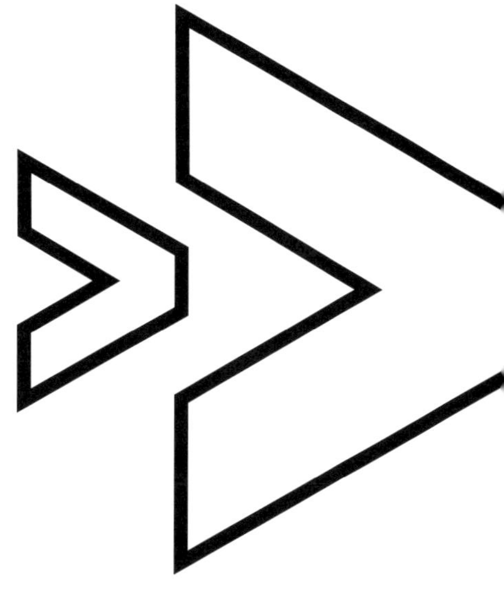

```
share /shâr/ n., v. [OHG scara (G Schar)
"troop"] [...] - v.t. 3. to divide and dis-
tribute in shares, apportions. 4. to use,
participate in, receive, etc., jointly:
"The two chemists shared the Nobel prize.
- v.i. 5. to have a share or part; take
part (in). 6. to receive equally.
```

From *Random House Webster's College Dictionary*

Sharing is a kind of relationship that goes beyond mere communication. It is said that early Christians recognized each other by bringing their faces close together and sniffing each other. One might say this sharing was extreme, entirely physical. They called this act "conspiracy." Fully sharing something, feeling part of something with others, is a form of conspiracy. Great architecture has always had a conspiratorial, engaging value; this architecture actually seems to come toward us, engaging us. How then can we give life to a shared language? In the not so distant past one of the obsessions of architects and artists was to create a more or less common language; in some cases they even intended to rebuild the world through a sharable intersubjective language. Without this ambition, much of modern art and architecture, and certainly its most heroic pages, cannot be explained. With the advent of postmodernity, this ambition was bracketed, or if nothing else communication has engulfed sharing. Italian architecture has provided notable examples of shared language. The many examples that have come down to us from the Middle Ages to the Baroque are characterized by the fact that they "conspire" with whoever experiences them. The action of time has clearly been decisive in ensuring the conspiracy take root, but this does not exempt us from the responsibility of creating new "co-inspirations" or at least new possibilities for sharing. There are several characteristics that distinguish sharing from communication. First and foremost is the fact that sharing does not communicate immediately; it does not try to capture attention at all costs. Spaces predisposed to sharing are not exciting and are sometimes even anonymous. Sharing also implies not just vision but the body as well. We share a space when we feel ourselves to be bodies (alone or with others) housed in a body or in what at this point we might call a body–architecture. This clearly involves relationships that are much more complex and articulated than those dictated by communication. It involves relationships that make shared spaces, when they are really such, capable of resisting their consumption. Thinking about it, it is almost impossible for a space in which sharing has truly taken hold to go out of style. There is still another characteristic that distinguishes communication and sharing, which is shared spaces' predisposition to ritual. The poet Cristina Campo wrote that a poetic action is such when it evokes a rite, a concept that can also be reiterated regarding Aldo Rossi's architecture. Ritual, as well known, is the instrument through which faiths and myths are perpetuated, and myths cannot exist without a founding act. Today's myth certainly cannot be that of past, absolute, sacred, written in letters of fire. Today's myths cannot be other than weak; they actually suit us better because they are not absolute. This does not mean that architecture cannot evoke a mythic atmosphere, in which a sense of an *epos*, of rooted collective narrative can be felt and perpetuated. All of this would seem far removed from politics, but it is not at all. Sharing is actually the founding act of democracy; it is or it should be the act that precedes action. Without sharing there would be no action; if this were not so it would reveal the presence of someone with dictatorial ambitions. Today, perhaps even more than before, the search for shared architecture is a political act in favor of democratic values.

Stories are meant to be shared, not at just one particular moment but over time. Ritual is born of this and with it myth. The shaft of Trajan's Column in Rome is enveloped and wrapped by epic events that rise toward the sky. Postmodernity has quite often avoided the epic tale and the drama it necessarily implies, hence all of it has slipped into irrelevance. In Masolino da Panicale's fresco, Saint Catherine stands in a room of clear geometric rigor arguing with the philosophers as she conveys her theses to them. Through the "modern" window on the right, the Saint can also be seen preaching. In Masolino's fresco, the story is doubled: it is shared with both the learned and the people.

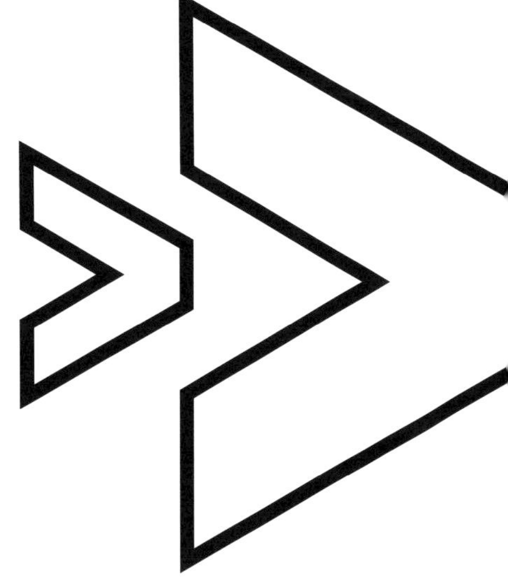

1. Trajan's Column, insert
   cover "Arte Romana," edited
   by Edoardo Persico in
   Domus, no. 96, 1935

2. Masolino da Panicale,
   *Saint Catherine's Disputation
   with the Philosophers of
   Alexandria*, 1428–30,
   Basilica of San Clemente,
   Rome

Sharing

A set of buildings that communicate with each other. In the project for the Italian Pavilion at Expo Dubai, the intention was to transform bodies into architecture in such a way that each figure became a building with its own character, its own posture, and its own temperament. In Piero della Francesca's fresco, the figures are different from yet similar to one another: among them, there is no duality between standing out and not standing out. Singularity in unity and unity in singularity: this seems to be the motto of Piero della Francesca's figures and architecture. By the means granted to us by analogy, all of this could be transmuted into an architectural landscape. We imagined individual buildings, well defined in their uniqueness, joined together by a bond that is spatial as well as figurative. It is a unusual landscape that defines a scene in which the figures turn toward the onlookers, almost as if they wanted to share the reasons for their being together with them.

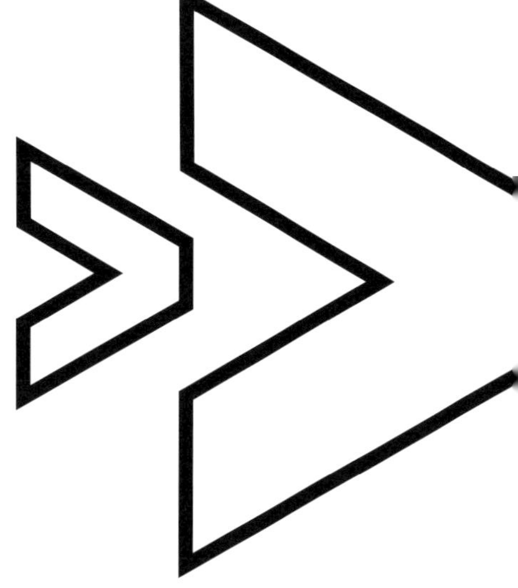

1. Project for the Italian
   Pavilion, Expo Dubai 2020

2. Piero della Francesca,
   *The Dream of Constantine,
   from the Legend of the
   True Cross*, Basilica of
   San Francesco, 1458–66,
   main chapel, Arezzo

1

Another lesson from Italian painting is that of not being afraid to represent popular forms, forms that are well defined in many people's imagination. The architecture represented in the fourteenth-century paintings of the Sienese School was similar to what could be seen in the city; similar, but not the same. In the hands of these painters, the architecture was stylized in such a way as to appear idealized, yet this idealization was always relative, always careful not to obscure the popular character the whole still had to maintain. There is a risk in using popular forms: if simply cited without any idealizing stylization, they can become didascalic and sometimes even kitsch. To ensure this does not happen, these popular icons have to be treated in such a way as to eliminate the populist potential they contain and can easily express at any moment. In the project for the expansion of the MAXXI in Rome, we tried to be popular without being populist.

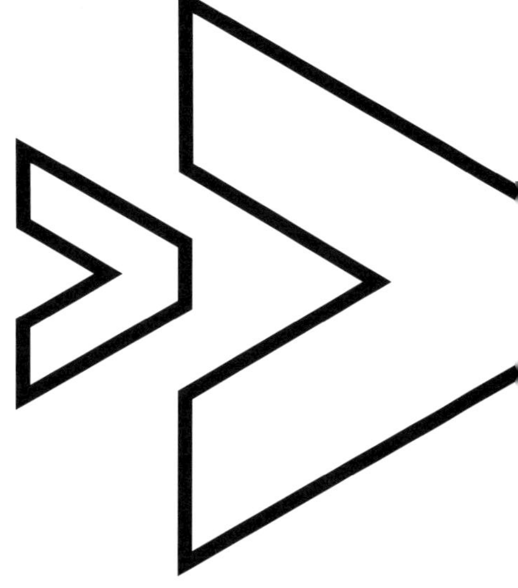

1. Project for the MAXXI
   expansion, archives and
   workshops, 2022, Rome

2. Luigi Ghirri, *Rimini*, 1977

E gli occhi aperti a guardare questa circostanza allo stesso tempo guardano. come quando sono aperti nel sogno. alla possibilità della sua trasformazione: il cammino dal punto di partenza del museo. punto fermo nella storia. verso l a venire. punto mobile e bersaglio incerto. si trascina dietro quel giubilante strepitio di forme e colori. come se le emozioni li contenute avessero la pretesa di continuare a vivere l'esterno. a esibirsi nelle loro contenute espressioni.

CIRCO COSMO
ZOO
CIRCO COSMO

Acting without being afraid of using a shared language, an evocative collective language. The circus often appears in twentieth-century Italian painting and film. It is the site of the exhilarating public event that, as such, is destined to be short-lived. The circus does not put down roots, it moves around; we are the ones who stay behind and wait for it to return. A museum made of circus tents, a museum that evokes what is popular and merry, the lights and sounds of celebration. The project for the expansion of the MAXXI in Rome drew inspiration from the circus tent to critique minimalist museums, rooted in respectability and in aseptic, pedantic clichés; the tent as an alternative to the sleek performance of design architecture. A museum that evokes what is sharable and does not exalt the affected sanctity of the world surrounding contemporary art.

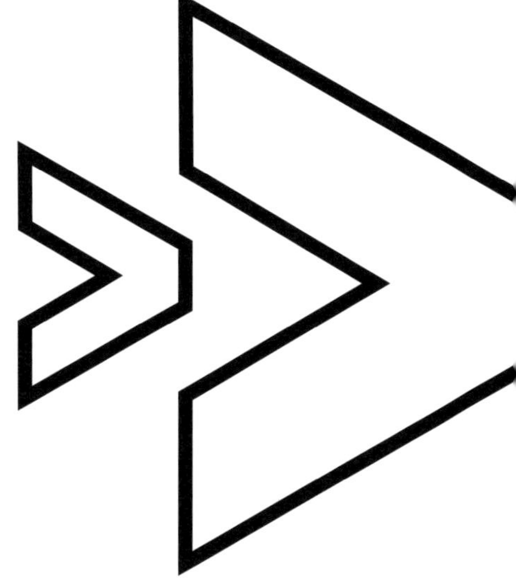

1. Carlo Carrà, *Festival*, 1924

2. Project for the MAXXI
   expansion, archives and
   workshops, 2022, Rome

To communicate, architecture often needs the support of graphics, of phrases that allow it to "speak." This brings to mind Boccioni's paintings, the ones in which, when pushing too far toward abstraction, he inserted letters and symbols, almost as if to curb the danger of slipping into pure self-referential composition. These enigmatic morphemes had the task of ensuring that the painting did not lose communication with the viewer. In the restoration of the large OGR industrial complex (the Officine Grandi Riparazioni di Torino), a project done in celebration of the 150th anniversary of Unification of Italy, we decided to expressly quote a painting by Osvaldo Licini in which a single black-and-white stripe is turned inward to occupy the center of the canvas. Painted on the ground in the project for Corte d'Onore, Licini's stripe has the role of defining the open space and, at the same time, of presenting itself as the building's primary identifying element. This project tried to find a crasis between communication and sharing by relying on Osvaldo Licini's work.

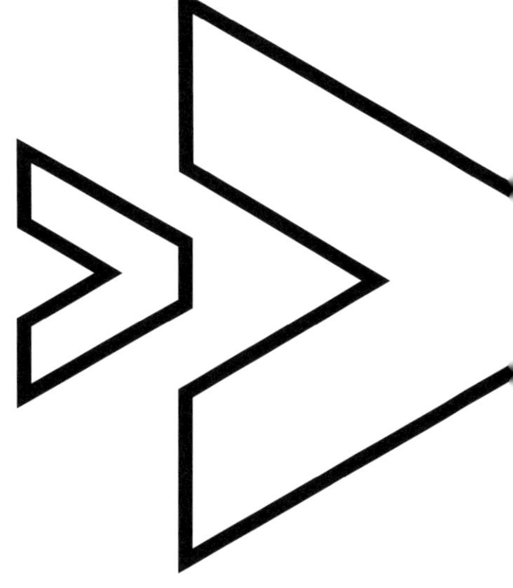

1. Osvaldo Licini,
   Composizione su fondo rosso
   [Composition on a Red
   Background], 1937

2. Officine Grandi Riparazioni
   Ferroviarie, 2011, Turin

S

In Piero della Francesca's *The Dream of Constantine* the emperor rests in a light suspended between night and day. He is protected by his soldiers and by the tent supported by a central pole. Tree and tent are two primary architectural elements, real archetypes of protection. These two archetypes are also complementary: the former is completely natural and supports; the latter is the fruit of human labor and is supported. The strength of Piero della Francesca's image also lies in the communicative capacity of these two primary building elements. Being rooted in myth, we recognize them immediately because they are ours deep down, in a depth that, among other, we share with others. Architecture's primary elements not only allow us to communicate, they also allow us to make images and spaces shareable.

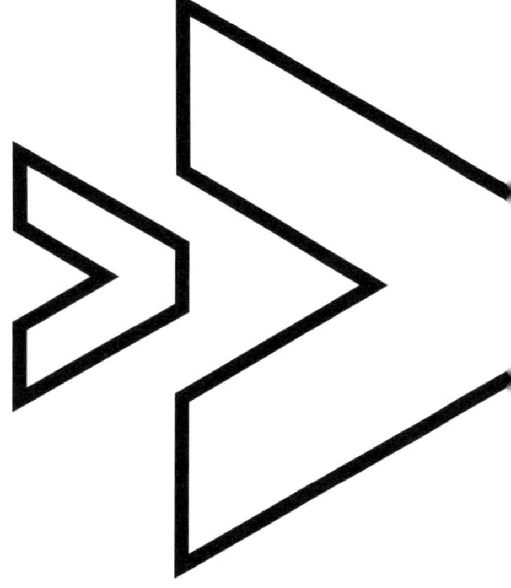

1. Project for the new parish
   of Sant'Ignazio da Laconi,
   2012, Olbia

2. *The Dream of Constantine,
   from the Legend of the
   True Cross*, Basilica of San
   Francesco, 1458–66, main
   chapel, Arezzo

# Sharing

In 1961 Michelangelo Antonioni shot the film *La Notte*, which, along with *L'Avventura* and *L'Eclisse*, is part of what was called, in Italian, the "trilogia dell'incomunicabilità" and, in English, the "trilogy of decadence" or the "the trilogy of modernity and its discontents" (*The Night–The Adventure–The Eclipse*). The characters in these three films are closed in on themselves, unable to open up to one another. They are unable to be alone and at the same time, as if under a spell, unable to be with others. The opening sequence of *La Notte* was shot in the Pirelli Tower in Milan while it was still under construction. The characters' incommunicability is mirrored in the icy building that celebrates Italy's entry into hopeful modernity. By the end of the film, however, the characters do open up to each other, they communicate and they do so by sharing their discomfort. In the film, we witness a catharsis: incommunicability is transcended by what is shared. This type of catharsis is not Antonioni's alone: it comes from twentieth-century Italian culture, a culture that, even in despair, has tried to never lose its sense of pietas.

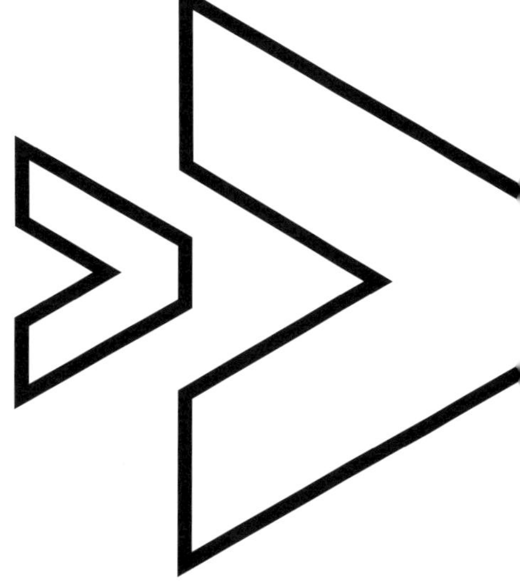

1. Michelangelo Antonioni,
   La Notte, still frame with
   Marcello Mastroianni and
   Monica Vitti, Italy 1961

2. Project for the school
   complex in Vado Ligure
   (Savona), 2020

Sharing

The central space of the Mausoleum of Santa Costanza in Rome is crowned by an ambulatory, the vault of which is frescoed with motifs from late Roman painting. The ambulatory is about half the height of the central space, and while the vault, though decorated, is dimly lit, the central space is bare and bright. The project for the new cruise terminal in the Port of Palermo proposed exporting, ideally outside, the mosaics of the ambulatory of Mausoleum of Santa Costanza. An attempt was made to create a public communicative space through the decorations of the canopies and a few characterizing architectural elements, such as the tree-like pillars that support the canopy itself.

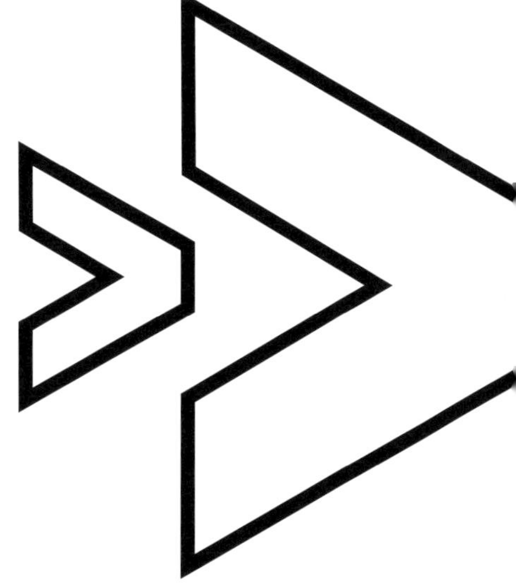

1. Mausoleum of Santa Costanza, detail of the ambulatory, 340–345 AD, Rome

2. Project for the new cruise terminal in port of Palermo and Ro-Ro, 2018

1

 Sharing

Renato Paresce's *Paesaggio* (1931) can be considered representative of a recurring theme in Italian painting in the 1930s: the enigma. Some have interpreted the enigma as the "rebus effect." The images represented by these painters were in fact similar to enigmatic puzzles in which people, objects, and landscapes appear clear and well defined in and of themselves, but the relationship between them is so completely indefinable it actually evokes a cryptic mystery. These painted rebuses communicated easily with viewers; they were accessible yet maintained a sense of enigma, something meant to elude us. The rebus effect can be used as a communication device for sharing what is represented; it is an expressive device that must be used cautiously to avoid lapsing into didacticism.

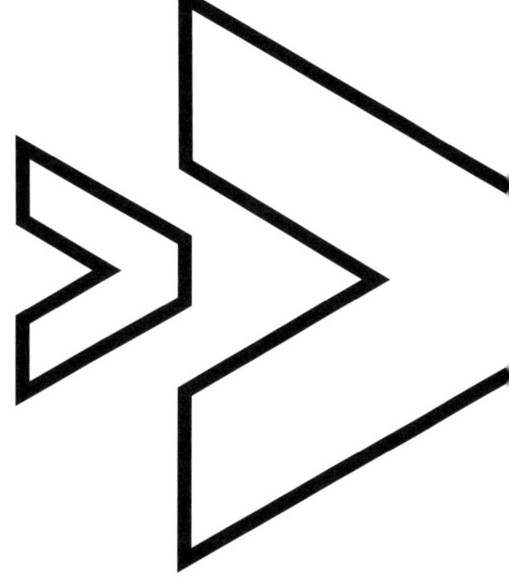

1. Renato Paresce, *Paesaggio* [Landscape], 1931

2. Project for the school complex in Vado Ligure (Savona), 2020

1

Sharing

In Ercole de Roberti's painting *Stories of Saint Vincent Ferrer*, a series of figures come in and out of various buildings that open and close in relation to them. The architecture depicted by Ercole de Roberti is porous, designed to be continuously interpenetrated. Sometimes it even goes so far as to become outdoor rooms, set no less on practically untilled land. In the project for the BEIC in Milan, an effort was made to create a building that was interpenetrable and therein both physically and functionally sharable.

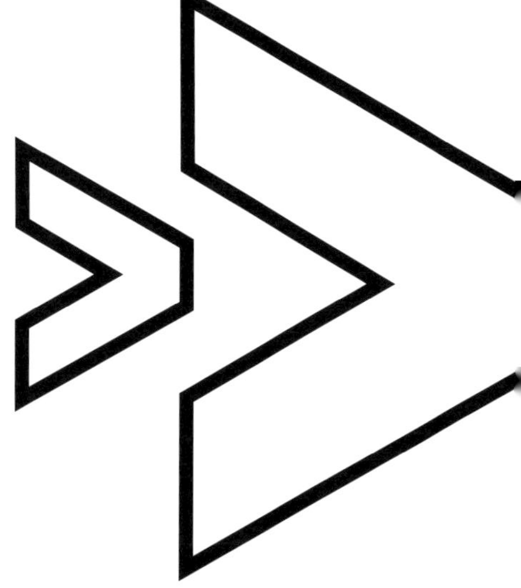

1. Ercole de' Roberti, *Stories of Saint Vincent Ferrer*, Polittico Griffoni, 1473, The Vatican Museums, Pinacoteca, Rome

2. Project for the new BEIC– Biblioteca Europea di Informazione e Cultura, 2022, Milan

1

2

Sharing

"This is the land of the resurrection, where one imagines finding one's friends, one's lovers after death."
(Albert Camus, Letter to Jean Grenier 1955)

Where are we? In Italy, yes, but when? *Quid Tum.* And now? And then? And so? The act of seeing strives to become an act of sharing. Looking at reality, however terrible it may be, is the destiny of an idea of architecture, body and space. Peluffo & Partners' projects aspire to be bodies that look at reality, at tragedy, at beauty, making all of this the object of sharing. Their architecture decides where to turn its gaze, how to look in order to see, what to turn its back to, whether to lie down or stand upright. It does not look citizens in the eye in an imposing way; it asks to be looked at, seen, and felt as it looks at the world.

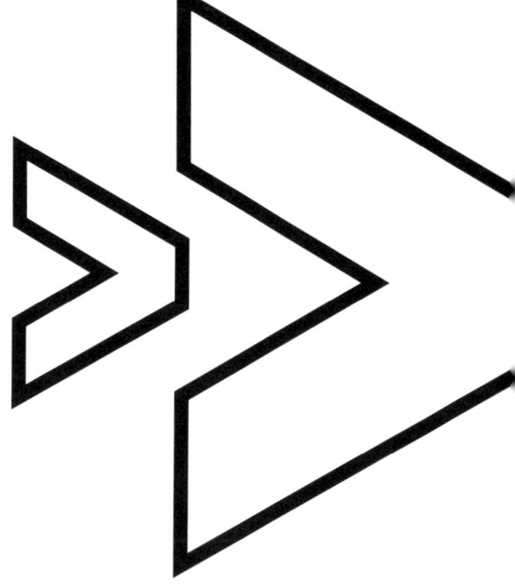

1. Roman bust, from the insert
   "Arte Romana," edited by
   Edoardo Persico in *Domus*,
   no. 96, 1935

2. Piero della Francesca,
   The Resurrection, detail,
   1458–68, Museo Civico,
   Sansepolcro

1

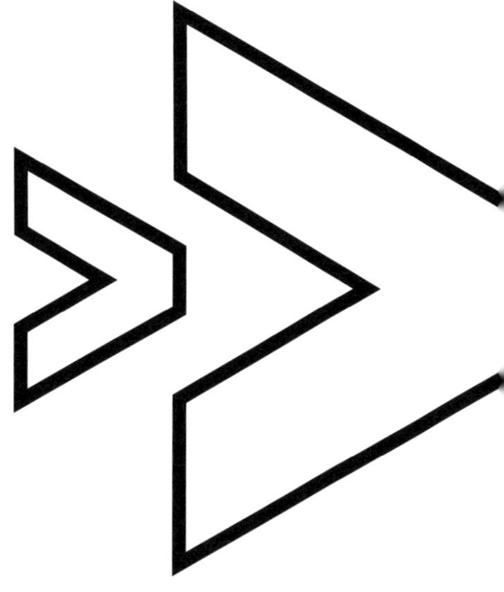

Clumsiness

clum•sy /klum'zē), adj. [ON lumsa lockjaw] 1.
Awkward in movement or action; lacking skill
or grace. —clum's•ily, adv. —clum'si•ness, n.

From *Random House Webster's College Dictionary*

Paul Klee was ambidextrous; although he was more skilled with his right hand, with which he wrote, he preferred to draw with his left. His choice was a question of technique: he actually wanted his painting to have a trace of imperfection, of what we might call skillful naïveté. Ultimately, he always wanted there be something clumsy in his work. It is surprising that Klee actually perfected this technique while he was working at the Bauhaus, the school that was teaching the art and design of machine civilization, or rather the polished aseptic perfection of infinitely reproducible objects. Clumsy does not mean poorly made, it does not mean unpolished or anything else. Clumsiness does not structure a form, if anything it adjectivizes it; it is like a spice that seasons a dish and, as such, can never replace it. As seen, the theme that recurs in this work and gives rise to it in its entirety is that of a-duality, of proposing a third way with respect to extreme, polarizing Manichean distinctions that represented the founding ideology of the modern movement. If, in Manichean fashion, we place perfection and imperfection, absolute finiteness and absolute informality at extremes, what we find in the middle, what mediates the two terms, is actually clumsiness. The architecture depicted by late medieval painters such as Cavallini and Giotto can be considered masterpieces of "clumsiness." The buildings look like architectural models made with skillful naïveté: the proportions are not perfectly respected, the architectural elements are often too thin, the facades sometimes disproportionate. The clumsiness and the skillful naïveté these works convey create a totally childlike atmosphere; clumsiness feeds on this and makes it visible. Modernity has taught us that this display of imperfection and childlike inexperience can become a political act. In the madness of World War I, Dada artists staged their childhood in their cabarets, flaunting it; it was an act of non-acceptance of the world as it was, of profound dissent, an existential dissent, joyful and desperate at the same time. After World War II, the philosopher Maurice Merleau-Ponty decided to change chairs at the Sorbonne, where he was teaching, moving from philosophy to "Child Psychology and Pedagogy." He was seeking the reasons for the expressive spontaneity of children's language, the language that comes before rational categorizations, the language of instinctive adherence to reality—a panic-like adherence out of which arise the myths that live in childhood imagination and poetic expression in general. If the perfect, proportionate, intelligible form is compared to the imperfect, clumsy form, it appears impenetrable, as if closed in itself, clearly hardly shareable. Clumsiness makes it possible to undermine this impenetrability, by mirroring our own totally human imperfection in its imperfection. We are now increasingly dominated by technical perfection. Once, in the machine age, this perfection was relative; the digital seems to have made it absolute today. In this context, clumsiness becomes an antagonistic form of expression in the face of the digital world. Clumsiness counters the aseptic, immaterial distance the digital imposes with physical adhesion to our surroundings. In the ceramic models with which some of their projects are represented, Peluffo & Partners has sought the means of expression suitable to the programmed imperfection we have called "clumsiness."

Clumsiness

Like many other artists of his time, the sculptor Arturo Martini was convinced that it was necessary to return to archaism. It was something Nietzsche, after all, had taught: the classical, that is the Apollonian form is nothing more than the sublimation, or transfiguration, of the archaic Dionysian form. The archaic form is hard, even harsh. There is nothing consoling about it in that it means to stage the natural brutality of things, their original tragic aspect. The Dionysian form does not intend to be perfect, or even perfectible. It is as though it were proud of its clumsy appearance in that this is what evokes the arcane of which it is a consequence. In its deliberate clumsiness, Brutalist architecture has sometimes managed to evoke a timeless past that is both archaic and modern. When it has distanced itself from this past, it has imploded in itself, falling back into the sterile game of forms incapable of evocation.

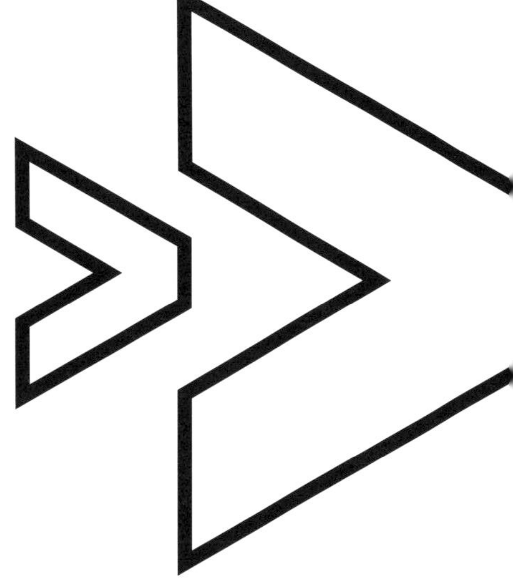

1. Arturo Martini, *Chimera*, 1934

2. Project for the new BEIC–Biblioteca Europea di Informazione e Cultura, 2022, Milan

Clumsiness

Mario Sironi's cityscapes are harsh. In them elemental buildings, devoid of anything that might make them graceful, stand out in an abandoned, suspended panorama, as if waiting for meaning. Sironi replaces the futurist clamor with an even more unsettling metaphysical stillness. The city, Sironi seems to say, develops on its own according to its own internal needs; then it is as if it stops and new landscapes appear imbued with their own unexpected, unmistakable character. His cityscapes seem to embody the fate of what is new in the city, the falling back into eternal return of which Nietzsche wrote. The IULM campus in Milan is located in the suburbs right outside the city, in the outskirts depicted by Boccioni and Sironi. The IULM buildings are purposefully anti-graceful. The few elements that characterize their facades are not perfectly in scale or coordinated with each other. At IULM there was an attempt to get past the extortion of good taste and composition, to break free of that design in which everything makes sense and nothing emerges.

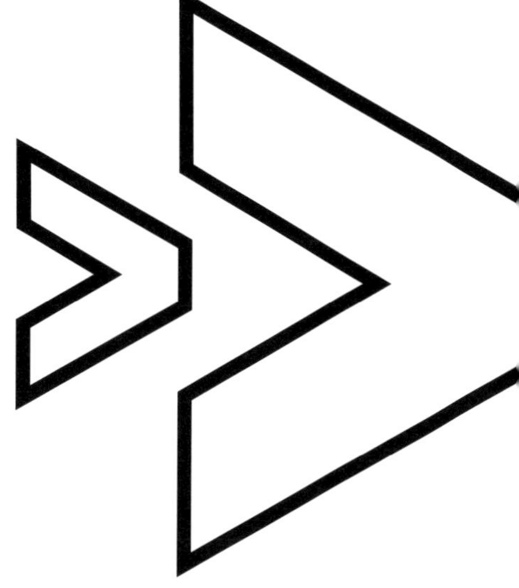

1. Mario Sironi, *Periferia,
   Il tram e la gru* [Outskirts,
   with tram and crane], 1921

2. IULM (University for
   Communications and
   Language) expansion,
   2015, Milan

Clumsiness

The painter Henry Rousseau, who was also known as "Le Douanier" (the customs officer), was self-taught and based his poetics on this. His painting is expressly naive, primary, devoid of any sophistication and any chiaroscuro. The contours of his figures are sharp, silhouetted, highlighted by broad swathes of color contained by the contours themselves. The proportions of his figures are by no means harmonious but by no means unpleasant: they are simply skillfully clumsy. It is actually this boyish, clumsy, expressive dimension that draws us to his painting. Nonetheless, Rousseau's painting is by no means vernacular; the enigmatic poses of his figures almost tend toward abstraction. One of the children in the school in Zugliano gave us drawing of his version of this place he knows so well: he drew it "Rousseau-style" deliberately respecting the building's somewhat awkward character. We like to interpret this as proof of how a dose of anti-gracefulness and clumsiness is essential to ensuring that architecture can be held in our unconscious.

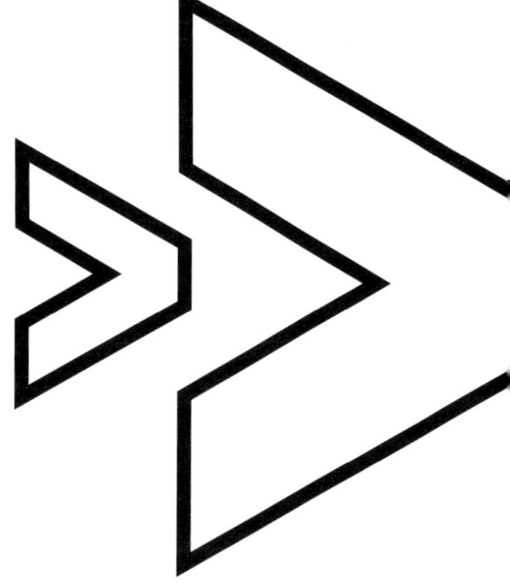

1. Henri Rousseau, *Myself, Portrait–Landscape*, 1889–90, National Gallery, Prague

2. Cover, "area," no. 146, reproducing a drawing by a student of the new school complex in Centrale, 2016

children
146
copenhagen itineraries
1

children
146
rivista internazionale di architettura e arti del progetto maggio/giugno 2016
essays Luca Molinari / Paolo Berardi / Paolo Peluffo / Alessandro Massarente / Massimo Malagugini interviews Paolo Crepet / Oliviero Toscani projects WORKac / Guillermo Hevia García, Nicolás Urzúa / Mareines + Patalano Arquitetura / Julio Barreno Gutiérrez / Graal Architecture / BASE / Dominique Coulon & associés / 5+1AA / Pietro Carlo Pellegrini with RCF & Partners / COBE / Verstas Architects / Ifat Finkelman + Deborah Warschawski / Coordination Asia / IROJE KHM Architects / Takahashi Ippei Office / copenhagen itineraries / bagnodesign surfaces / design focus colors

Clumsiness

In the 1930s Campari hired the Futurist artist Fortunato Depero to revamp its brand and its communication. Depero was not used by Campari; on the contrary, Campari is used by the artist to overturn the expressive practices of what is now called branding. In his ads, Depero does not exalt the Campari brand; he uses it as a tool to evoke a simpler, happier everyday life. Through the drink, he gives life to a world that is finally shaking off the alluring sentimentality of Art Nouveau. In doing so, he uses a lively, wry, anti-gracious language, a language that is analogous to the jazz that was then taking hold. With his ads, Depero discovered new modes of expression that might be really helpful today in finally challenging the prevailing ideology of the perfect, aseptic, aphasic form.

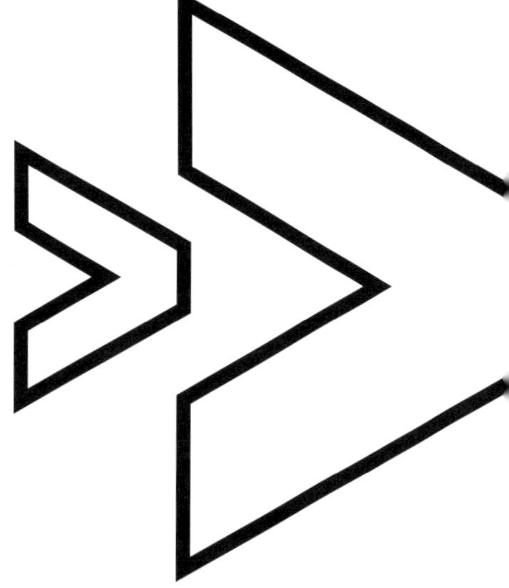

1. Fortunato Depero, Campari
   advertisement, 1928

2. Beniamino Servino, insert
   cover for "La Lettura"
   in *Corriere della Sera*,
   reproduction of a sketch
   of "The Stone" residential
   building, 2023

CAMPARI
F. Depero
1

BS 09 07 2023
CORRIERE DELLA SERA
la Lettura
THREE PEAKS YELLOW STONE
CORRIERE DELLA SERA

Clumsiness

In the predella of the polyptych dedicated to Blessed Novello, Simone Martini recounts the miracle performed by the Saint, who saves a child falling from the balcony. The scene is frantic, the figures are agitated and flailing their arms at the Saint's arrival from above; they are clearly over the top. The buildings that make up the scene seem to mimic their commotion; they appear ungainly, clearly clumsy. Yet despite this, their excitement is not completely extroverted; it does not coincide with that of the figures. The buildings depicted by Simone Marini actually appear restrained, and it is this relative composure that makes them unobtrusive, that keeps them from being "ugly." Clumsiness is an expressive dimension that can never be radical; it cannot place itself definitely outside the lines that define the canons of good taste, if anything it has to be placed within them. Clumsiness can be likened to a spice that can make a dish unique but can never replace it.

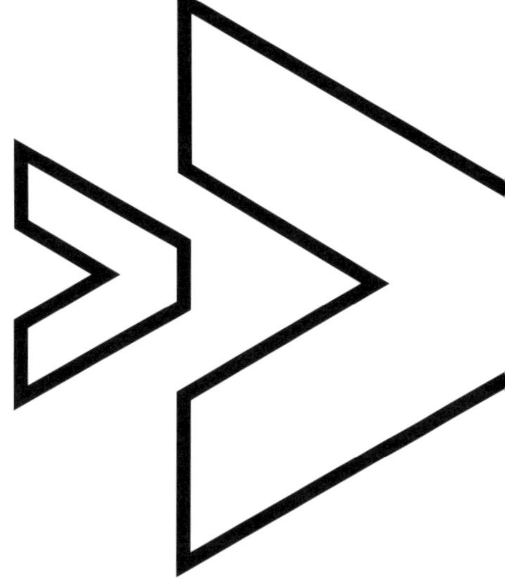

1. Simone Martini, *Blessed
   Agostino Novello Altarpiece*,
   1324, Pinacoteca Nazionale,
   Siena

2. Ceramic model of the
   project for the Italian
   Pavillion, Expo Dubai 2020

Clumsiness

In 1966 Paolo Portoghesi presented one of his most seductive projects, the apartment tower in Santa Marinella. The idea was that of a tower composed of nothing more than an apparently totally random vertical stacking of what looked like ordinary, ungainly shacks. Portoghesi's heretical project ennobles so-called spontaneous languages to the highest degree, and it does so without populism or irritating social-political intentions. The lopsided, the incomplete, the random, the rough, and the unfinished come together in a masterpiece project of twentieth-century clumsiness. By analogy, memory goes to the terra-cotta model we studied for the ceiling of the mosque on the Galala Mountain, it too poised between clumsy spontaneous languages and the rules of higher languages.

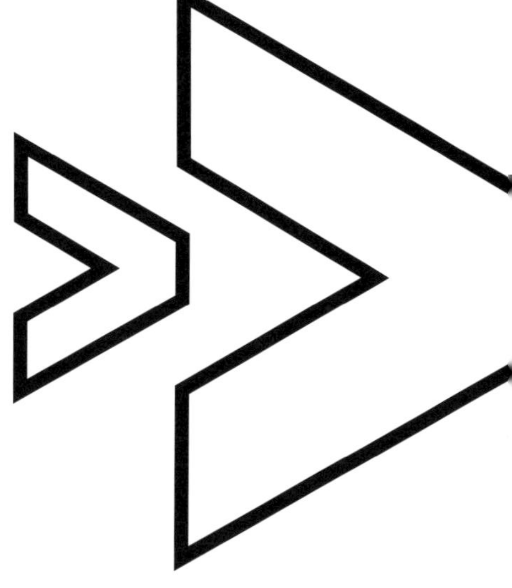

1. Paolo Portoghesi, project for
   an apartment tower in Santa
   Marinella (Rome), 1966

2. Mosque in Sokhna, 2019–
   in progress, Monte Galala,
   Egypt

Clumsiness

Ruins are clumsy: they are imperfect bodies, corroded by time, proudly bearing the effects of time itself; a polished ruin would actually be a contradiction. In writing about Byzantine architecture, Bruno Zevi noted that its charm lay in its capacity to evoke ruins on the exterior, an evocation that was further reinforced by the glittering mosaics inside. In this regard, Zevi wrote of "shimmering walls," of walls that vibrate in the light because of their imperfection. They are tactile walls that can express the grain of the material and its texture, sincerely clumsy walls that appear supplanted today by the visual, embodied walls of design architecture. The shimmering walls described by Bruno Zevi were the reference for the nursery school project in Vado Ligure.

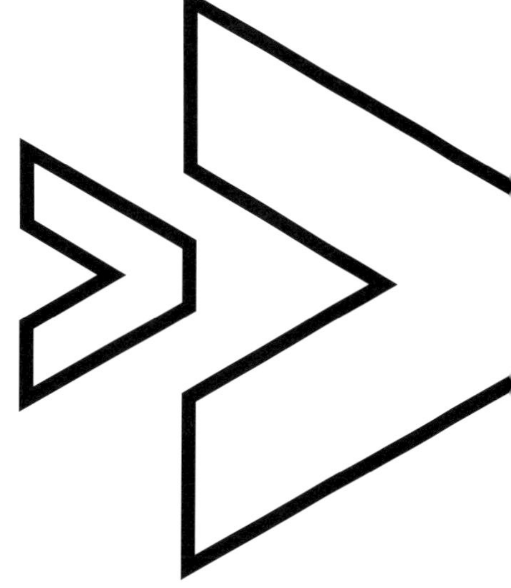

1. Project for the nursery
   school in the Vado Ligure
   school complex, Savona,
   2020

2. Umbilicus urbis Romae,
   second century BC–150
   AD, Archaeological Park of
   the Colosseum, Roman
   Forum, Rome

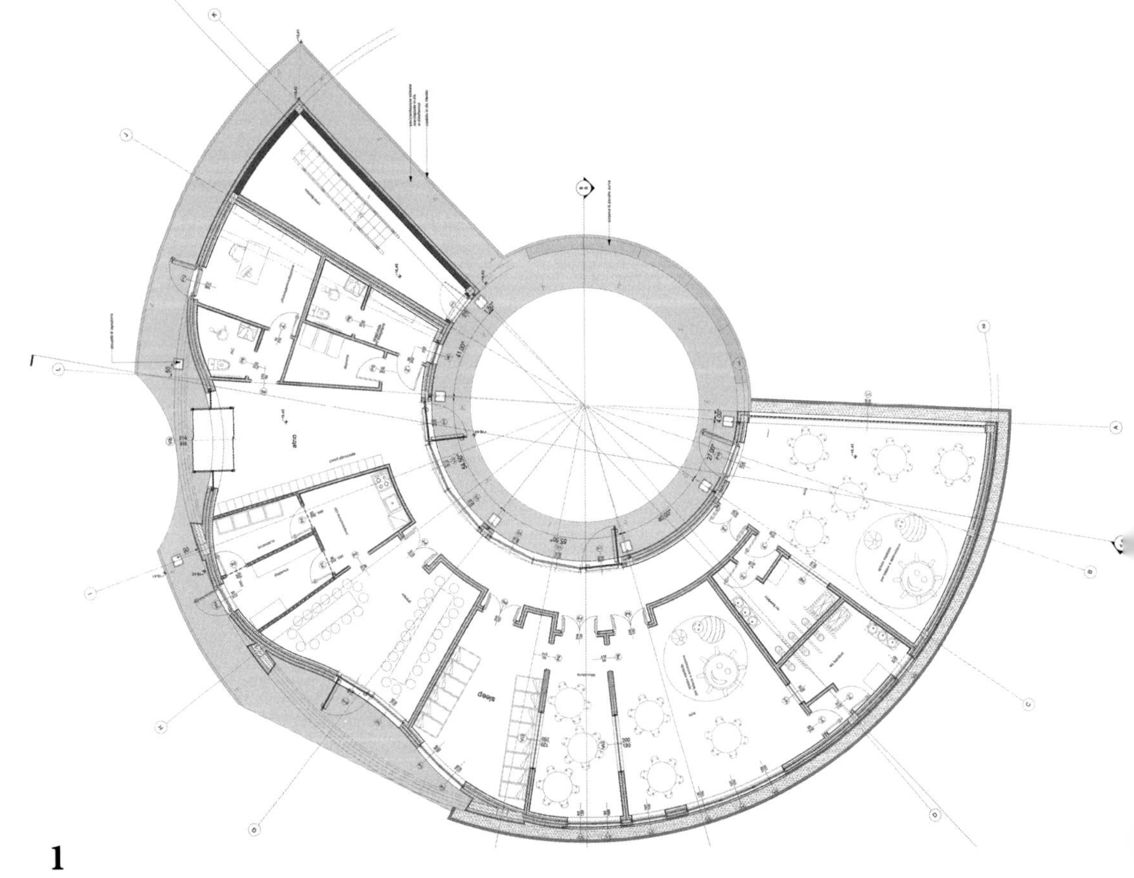

1

Clumsiness

The city is made of chasms. In the project for the BEIC in Milan, the idea of continuity between the public space, park, and building translates into an unnatural twisting of an architectural body. This poses a challenge that leads to breaking one's back in an awkward, almost desperate tension—a tension intent on revealing the reality of a city that, like a fallen animal, tries to emit a desperate cry for the future and sociality. Arturo Martini translates the drama of the fallen Pegasus into the heroic beauty of the body—the front legs accept the drama while the desperate hind legs and head rebel.

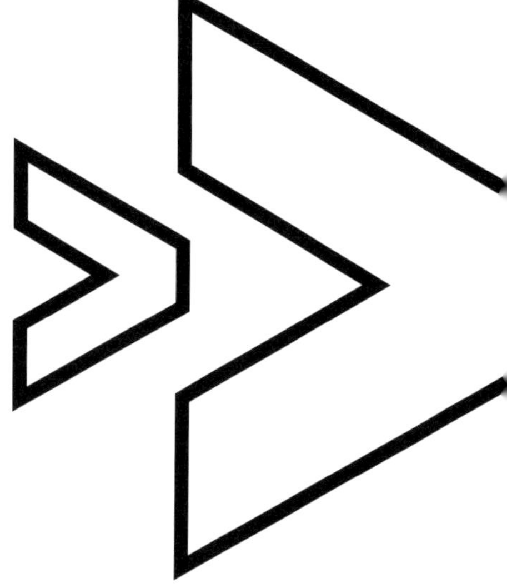

1. Project for the new BEIC–
   Biblioteca Europea di
   Informazione e Cultura,
   2022, Milan

2. Photo of Arturo Martini's
   Fallen Pegaso, replica of the
   original plaster, 1963, Vado
   Ligure (Savona)

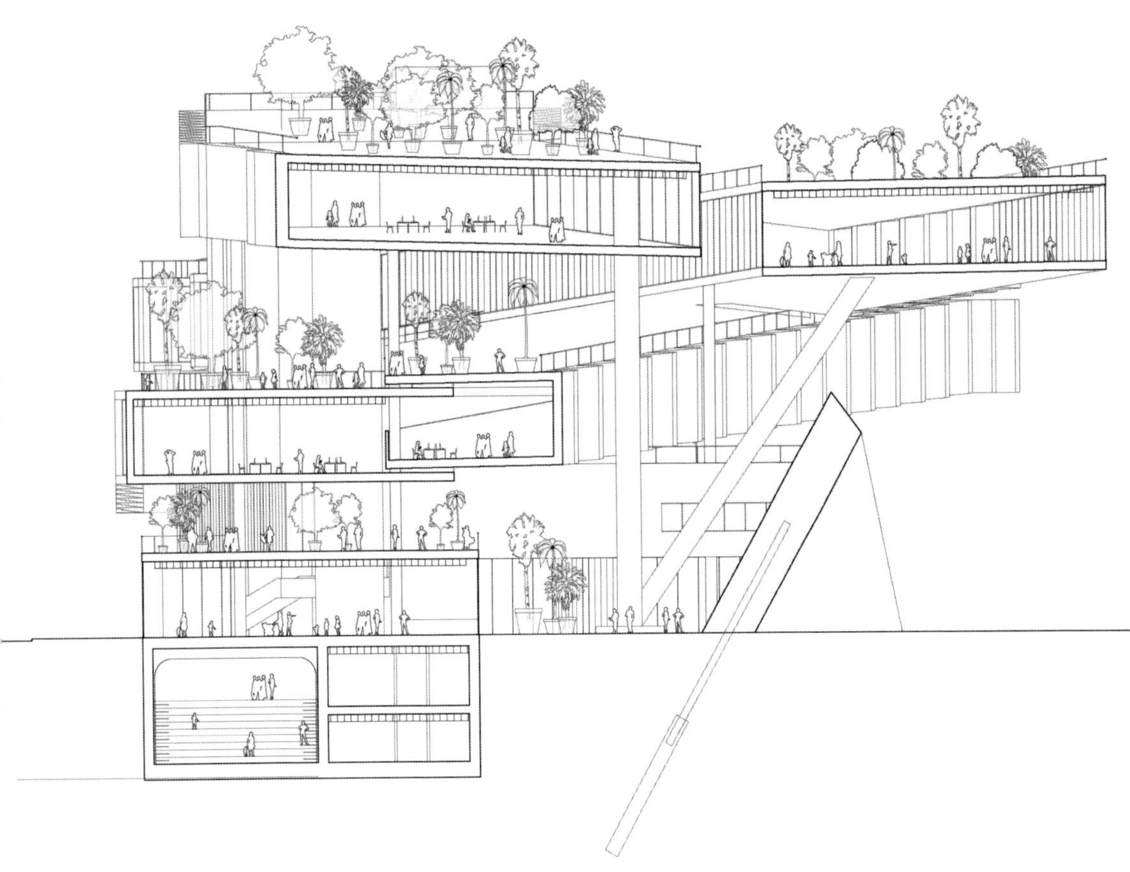

1

Giovanni Michelucci, church of San
Giovanni Battista, interior, 1960–64,
Florence

Bibliography:

Giorgio Agamben, *Cosa è il contemporaneo* (Milan: Nottetempo, 2008). English ed. *What is an apparatus? And Other Essays*, translated by David Kishik and Stefan Pedatella (Red Wood City, CA: Stanford University Press, 2009).

Giorgio Agamben, *Gusto* (Macerata: Quodlibet, 2015). English ed. *Taste*, translated by Cooper Francis (New York-Calcutta-London: Seagull Books, 2017).

Fernando Amigoni, *Il metodo Mimetico-Realistico* (Bari: Laterza, 2001).

Francis Bacon, *La brutalità delle cose. Conversazioni con David Sylvester* (Casarsa della Delizia: Quaderni Pier Paolo Pasolini, 1991). See David Sylvester, *Interviews with Francis Bacon* (London: Thames and Hudson, 1985).

Roland Barthes, *La camera chiara* (Turin: Einaudi, 1980). English ed. *Camera Lucida: Reflections on Photography*, translated by Richard Howard (New York: Hill and Wang, 1981).

Charles Baudelaire, *Scritti sull'arte* (Turin: Einaudi, 2014). English ed. *Selected Writings on Art & Artists*, translated by P.E. Charvet (Cambridge: Cambridge University Press, 1981).

Umberto Boccioni, *Diari* (Milan: Abscondita, 2003).

Fernand Braudel, *Il Mediterraneo* (Milan: Bompiani, 1985). English ed. *Memory and the Mediterranean* (New York: Knopf Doubleday Publishing Group, 2002).

Cristina Campo, *Gli imperdonabili* (Milan: Adelphi, 1987).

Albert Camus, *L'estate e altri saggi solari* (Milan: Bompiani, 2019). English ed. *Lyrical and Crytical Essays*, translated by Ellen Conroy Kennedy (New York: Alfred A. Knopf, 1968).

François Cheng, *Cinque meditazioni sulla bellezza* (Turin: Bollati Boringhieri, 2006). English ed. *Way of Beauty. Five Meditations for Spiritual Transformation*, translated by Jody Gladding (Rochester, VT – Toronto: Inner Traditions, 2009).

Benedetto Croce, *Breviario di estetica. Aestetica in nuce* (Milan: Adelphi, 1990). English ed. *Aesthetic as Science of Expression and General Linguistic*, edited and translated by Colin Lyas (Cambridge: Cambridge University Press, 1992).

T.S. Eliot, *Cosa è classico* in Idem, *Opere* (Milan: Bompiani, 1992). English ed. *Selected Essays* (London: Faber & Faber, 1999).

Pavel Florensky, *Lo spazio e il tempo* (Milan: Adelphi, 1995).

Pavel Florensky, *Le porte regali. Saggio sull'icona* (Milan: Adelphi, 2021). English ed. *Beyond Vision. Essays on the Perception of Art*, compiled and edited by Nicoletta Misler, translated by Wendy Salmond (London: Reaktion Books, 2002).

Roberto Galasso, *Il rosa Tiepolo* (Milan: Adelphi, 2018). English ed. *Tiepolo Pink*, translated by Alastair McEwen (New York City: Penguin Books, 2020).

Ernst H. Gombrich, *L'immagine e l'occhio* (Turin: Einaudi, 1985). English ed. *The Image and the Eye. Further Studies in the Psycology of Pictorial Representation* (Oxford: Phaidon, 1982).

Ernst H. Gombrich, *Arte, percezione e realtà* (Turin: Einaudi, 2002).

Ernst H. Gombrich, Luca Biasioni, ed., *La preferenza per il primitivo. Episodi della storia del gusto e dell'arte occidentale* (Turin: Einaudi, 2023). English ed. *The Preference for the Primitive* (Oxford: Phaidon, 2002).

Romano Guardini, *Lettere dal lago di Como. La tecnica e l'uomo* (Brescia: Morcelliana, 1993). English ed. *Letters from Lake Como. Explorations in Technology and Human Race*, translated by Geoffrey W. Bromiley (Grand Rapids: William B. Eerdams Publishing, 1994).

James Hillman, *Politica della Bellezza* (Bergamo: Moretti e Vitali, 1999).

James Hillman, *L'anima dei luoghi* (Milan: Rizzoli, 2004).

Ernst Jünger, *Foglie e pietre* (Milan: Adelphi, 1997). English ed. *Leaves and Stones*, (Stuggart: Klett-Cotte Verlag, 1978).

Ernst Jünger, *Al muro del tempo* (Milan: Adelphi, 2000).

Paul Klee, *Diari. 1898-1918* (Milan: Il Saggiatore, 2018). English ed. *Diaries of Paul Klee 1898-1918*, with an introduction by Felix Klee (Los Angeles: University of California Press, 1992).

Roberto Longhi, *"Gli affreschi del Carmine, Masaccio e Dante"* in: *Da Cimabue a Morandi. Saggi di storia della pittura italiana scelti e ordinati da Gianfranco Contini* (Milan: Mondadori, 1973).

Roberto Longhi, *Piero della Francesca* (Milan: Abscondita, 2004).

Roberto Longhi, *Breve ma veridica storia della pittura italiana* (Milan: Abscondita, 2018).

Maurice Merleau-Ponty, *Fenomenologia della percezione* (Milan: Il Saggiatore, 1965). English ed. *Phenomenology of Perception*, translated by Donald A. Landes (New York City: Routledge, 2012).

Maurice Merleau-Ponty, *La Prosa del Mondo* (Rome: Editori riuniti, 1984). With an introduction by Carlo Sini. English ed. *The Prose of the World*, edited by Claude Lefort, translated by John O'Neill (London: Northwestern University Press, 1973).

Maurice Merleau-Ponty, Mauro Carbone, ed., *Il visibile e l'invisibile* (Milan: Bompiani, 1999). English ed. *The Visible and the Invisible*, edited by Claude Lefort, translated by Alphonso Lingis (London: Northwestern University Press, 1968).

Valerio P. Mosco, *L'ultima cattedrale* (Genoa: Sagep, 2015).

Valerio P. Mosco, *Kitsch in architettura* (Siracusa: LetteraVentidue, 2023).

Novalis, *Frammenti* (Milan: Rizzoli, 1981). English ed. *Pollen and Fragments*, translated and introduction by Arthur Verluis (Milan: Phanes Press, 1989).

Walter F. Otto, *Il volto degli dei* (Rome: Fazi, 2016).

Octavio Paz, *L'apparenza nuda. L'opera di Marcel Duchamp* (Milan: Abscondita, 2019). English ed. *Marcel Duchamp. Appearance Stripped Bare*, translated (New York City: Skyhorse, 2011).

Gianluca Peluffo, *Il Giuramento di Pan* (Venice: Marsilio, 2021).

Paolo Portoghesi, Giovanna Massobrio, *L'immaginario architettonico nella pittura* (Bari: Laterza, 1988).

Carlo L. Ragghianti, *Arti della visione. III. Il linguaggio critico* (Torino: Einaudi, 1979).

Aldo Rossi, *Autobiografia scientifica* (Milan: Il Saggiatore, 2023). English ed. *A Scientific Autobiography*, translated by Lawrence Venuti (Boston, Boston MIT Press, 2010).

Arthur Schopenhauer, Eleonora Caramelli, ed., *Metafisica del bello* (Milan: Aesthetica, 2022). English ed. *Schopenhauer: Parerga and Paralipomena: Vol. 2*, edited by Christopher Janaway (Cambridge: Cambridge University Press, 2015).

Roger Scruton, *La bellezza. Ragione ed esperienza estetica* (Milano: Vita e Pensiero, 2010). English ed. *Beauty: a very short introduction* (Oxford: Oxford University Press, 2011).

Hans Sedlmayr, *Perdita del centro* (Rome: Borla, 1967). English ed. *Art in Crisis. The Lost Centre*, translated by Brian Battershaw (New York City: Routledge, 2017).

Jean Starobinski, *1789. I sogni e gli incubi della ragione* (Milan: Garzanti, 1981).

Andrea Tagliapietra, *I cani del tempo. Filosofia e icone della pazienza* (Rome: Donzelli, 2022).

Eugenio Turri, *Il Paesaggio come Teatro* (Venice: Marsilio, 2010).

Lionello Venturi, *Il gusto dei primitivi* (Turin: Einaudi, 1972).

Anthony Vidler, *Il perturbante in Architettura. Saggi sul disagio dell'età contemporanea* (Turin: Einaudi, 2006). English ed. *The Architectural Uncanny*, (Boston: MIT Press, 1992)

Paul Virilio, *Città panico* (Milan: Raffaello Cortina Editore, 2004). English ed. *City of Panic, translated by Julie Rose* (Oxford: Berg, 2004).

Simone Weil, Concetta Sala, ed., *La persona e il sacro* (Adelphi, Milano, 2012).

Luigi Zoja, *Giustizia e Bellezza* (Turin: Bollati Boringhieri, 2007).

Credits:

**Seafood market and public
spaces in Trapani
(p. 28)**

Scope: international competition,
2021 – winner
City: Trapani, Italy
Status: ongoing, 2021–under
construction
Architectural project: Peluffo& Partners,
Valle 3.0, Marco Antonini Architects,
Carmen Andriani, Vito Corte
Structural project: Technital
Area: 8,545 sqm
Costs: 20,864,400 €
Client: Autorità del Sistema Portuale
del Mare di Sicilia Occidentale

**Italian pavilion Expo Dubai 2020
(pp. 32, 176)**

Scope: international competition,
2019 – winner
City: Dubai, Arab Emirates
Status: project
Architectural project: Peluffo & Partners,
Fondazione Symbola, HZ Studio –
Architecture & Engeenering srl,
Green Land srl
Structural project: PRAS Tecnica DiLisio
srl Società Ingegneria
Area: 35,000 sqm
Costs: 26,000,000 €
Client: Invitalia

**Reuse of ex-Caserma Ferdinando di
Savoia – Ministero degli Interni
(pp. 37, 107)**

City: Rome, Italy
Status: completed, 2003–09
Architectural project: Peluffo & Partners
Dimensions: 43,840 sqm
Costs: 67,500,000 €
Client: Ministero delle Infrastrutture e
dei Trasporti – SAC spa

**Project for the El Alamein
Battle Museum
(p. 40)**

Intervention: construction of a
museum commemorating the Battle
of El Alamein (1942)
City: El Alamein, Egypt
Status: project
Architectural project: Peluffo & Partners
Costs: reserved
Client: Ministry of Housing and New
urban Communities of Egypt

**Restoration of the Marseille Docks
(p. 45)**

Intervention: restoration of the historical
complex
Status: completed, 2009–15
City: Trapani, Italy
Architectural project: Gianluca Peluffo
with 5+1AA
Dimensions: 21,000 sqm
Costs: 21,000,000 €
Client: JP Morgan, Constructa

New A.S.I. (Italian Space Agency) headquarters
(pp. 49, 123, 135)

Intervention: construction of an office building and additional services
City: Rome, Italy
Status: completed, 2007–12
Architectural project: Gianluca Peluffo with 5+1AA
Dimensions: 28,600 sqm
Costs: 35,000,000 €
Client: Ministero delle Infrastrutture e dei Trasporti Servizio Integrato Infrastrutture e Trasporti per il Lazio, l'Abruzzo e la Sardegna

Project for the Lapis Niger Area
(p. 53)

Intervention: redesign of the access and coverage area of the archaeological site
City: Rome (Foro Romano), Italy
Status: ongoing, 2022–under construction
Architectural project: Peluffo & Partners
Structural project: Lamoureux – Ricciotti ingegneri, VP6 ingegneria
Dimensions: 720 sqm
Costs: 3,300,000 €
Client: Parco Archeologico del Colosseo

Nautical Institute of Gallipoli
(p. 57)

Scope: international competition, 2020
City: Gallipoli, Italy
Status: project
Architectural project: Peluffo & Partners, MAS – Modern Apulian Style
Dimensions: 3,570 sqm
Costs: 9,878,348 €
Client: Sviluppo Sistema Fiera spa

Project for the Biblioteca di Lettere, Sapienza University of Rome
(p. 61)

Scope: international competition, 2022
City: Rome, Italy
Status: project
Architectural project: Peluffo & Partners, Alterstudio Partners, FORMEstudio
Systems project: E-Plus studio
Dimensions: 13,000 sqm
Costs: 16,500,000 €
Client: La Sapienza University

Project for "The Stone," a residential building
(p. 75)

Intervention: realization of a new residential building
City: Cervinia, Italy
Status: ongoing, 2022–under construction
Architectural project: Peluffo & Partners
Structural project: VP6 Ingegneria
Dimensions: 2,700 sqm
Costs: 5,400,000 €
Client: Vico srl

**Project for the Science Museum
in Rome
(p. 79)**

Scope: international competition, 2023
City: Rome, Italy
Status: project
Architectural project: Peluffo & Partners,
Studio Azzurro, Prof. Arch. Orazio
Carpenzano, Arch. Fabio Balducci,
Arch. Paolo Marcoaldi
Structural project: Compass
Engeenering
Dimensions: 19,300 sqm
Costs: 38,600,000 €
Client: Municipality of Rome

**Project for the Ospedale
degli Incurabili
(pp. 83, 139)**

Intervention: requalification,
restauration e refunctionalization of the
monumental complex of Santa Maria del
Popolo degli Incurabili in Naples.
Scope: international competition, 2020
City: Naples, Italy
Status: project
Architectural project: Peluffo & Partners
with Prof. Arch. Orazio Carpenzano,
Studio Dismisura
Structural project: Binini Partners
Dimensions: 32,000 sqm
Costs: 65,000,000 €
Client: Azienda Sanitaria Locale Napoli
1 Centro

**Project for the new parish
of Sant'Ignazio da Laconi
(pp. 87, 192)**

Intervention: design of the new
parish complex comprising the
church, the rectory and the premises
for pastoral ministry
Scope: international competition, 2012
– winner
City: Olbia, Italy
Status: project
Architectural project: Gianluca Peluffo
with 5+1AA
Artistic collaborations:
Claudio Parmiggiani
Dimensions: 8,243 sqm
Costs: 4,250,000 €
Client: Conferenza Episcopale
Italiana (CEI) with the diocese of
Tempio Ampurias

**Horizontal Tower
(p. 91)**

Intervention: realization of new
management structures for Fiera Milano
Scope: international competition,
2008 – winner
City: Milan, Italy
Status: completed, 2008–14
Architectural project: Gianluca Peluffo
with 5+1AA, Jean-Baptiste Pietri
Construction company:
Italiana Costruzioni
Dimensions: 12,000 sqm
Costs: 32,000,000 €
Client: Sviluppo Sistema Fiera spa

**Project for the new school
complex in Centrale
(pp. 95, 155)**

City: Zugliano (Vicenza), Italy
Status: completed, 2010–15
Architectural project: Gianluca Peluffo
with Diego Peruzzo, 5+1AA
Dimensions: 2,500 sqm
Costs: 4,200,000 €
Client: Municipality of Zugliano

**Project for the school complex
in Vado Ligure
(pp. 98, 205)**

Scope: international competition,
2020–21
City: Vado Ligure (Savona), Italy
Status: project
Architectural project: Peluffo & Partners
Structural project: VP6 Ingegneria
Dimensions: 2,500 sqm
Costs: 5,200,000 €
Client: Municipality of Vado Ligure
Ceramic model: La casa dell'arte in
Albissola Capo by Danilo Trogu with
Gianluca Peluffo

**Mosque in Sokhna
(pp. 103, 115)**

City: Ain Sokhna, Egypt
Status: ongoing, 2019–under
construction
Architectural project: Peluffo & Partners
Dimensions: 3,400 sqm
Costs: reserved
Client: Tatweer Misr

**Project for a rest and service area
(p. 111)**

Intervention: architectural
and landscape design of a service
and rest area
Scope: international competition,
2018 – 3rd prize
City: Sarzamin, Iran
Status: project
Total area: 46,000 sqm
Architectural project: Peluffo & Partners
with Flavio Mangione Architetto,
Hossein Mahoutipour

**IULM (University for
Communications and Language)
expansion
(pp. 119, 227)**

City: Milan, Italy
Status: completed, 2003–15
Architectural project: Gianluca Peluffo
con 5+1AA
Dimensions: 9,950 sqm

**Project for the L. Ghiberti
School in Pelago
(p. 142)**

Scope: international competition PNRR
Scuola Futura 2022, 2020 – winner
City: Pelago (Florence), Italy
Status: project
Architectural project: Peluffo & Partners,
ARX srl
Structural project: VP6 Ingegneria
Dimensions: 3,500 sqm
Costs: 6,000,000 €
Client: Municipality of Pelago

**New BNL Paribas
headquarters in Rome
(p. 147)**

City: Rome, Italy
Status: completed, 2012–16
Architectural project: Gianluca Peluffo
with 5+1AA
Dimensions: 75,000 sqm
Costs: 83,000,000 €
Client: BNP Paribas Real Estate
Development spa

**Project for the main field
of the Foro Italico
(p. 151)**

Scope: international competition, 2020
City: Rome, Italy
Status: project
Architectural project: Peluffo & Partners,
Rudy Ricciotti with Prof. Arch. Orazio
Carpenzano
Dimensions: 16,000 sqm
Costs: 27,588,650 €
Client: Sport e salute spa

**Ex Opificio D'Oria
(p. 158)**

Intervention: renovation in a 16th
century building
City: Loano (Savona), Italy
Status: completed, 2008
Architectural project: Antonio Lagorio,
Peluffo & Partners founding partner
Dimensions: 200 sqm
Client: private

**Monte Galala New Town
(p. 162)**

Intervention: elaboration of the
masterplan for a residential city
City: Ain Sokhna, Egypt
Status: ongoing, 2015–under
construction
Architectural project: Peluffo & Partners
Dimensions: 1,300,000 sqm
Costs: 1,568,655,208.80 €
Client: Tatweer Misr

**Project for the MAXXI expansion,
archives and workshops
(pp. 180, 185)**

Scope: international competition, 2022
City: Rome, Italy
Status: project
Architectural project: Peluffo & Partners,
Beniamino Servino, Elasticospa
Dimensions: 4,800 sqm
Costs: 14,200,000 €
Client: MAXXI – Museo nazionale delle
arti del XXI secolo

**Project for Officine Grandi
Riparazioni Ferroviarie
(p. 189)**

Intervention: conversion into
a multifunctional space
Scope: international competition,
2009 – winner
City: Turin, Italy
Status: completed, 2009-11
Architectural project: Gianluca Peluffo
with Studio Azzurro, 5+1AA,
Studio Pession

Collaborations: Danilo Trogu
Dimensions: 24,500 sqm
Costs: 10,000,000 €
Client: Municipality of Firenze

**Project for the new cruise terminal
in port of Palermo and Ro-Ro
(p. 201)**

Scope: international competition,
2018 – runner-up
City: Palermo, Italy
Status: project
Architectural project: Peluffo & Partners,
ARX progettazione
Structural project: Milan Ingegneria srl
Dimensions: 300,000 sqm
Costs: 70,300,000 € (expected amount)
Client: Port Authority of Palermo

**Project for the new BEIC – Biblioteca
Europea di Informazione e Cultura
(pp. 208-209, 223)**

City: Milan, Italy
Status: completed, 2022
Architectural project: Peluffo & Partners,
Altestudio Partners
Structural project: Tecnicaer
Engineering srl
Landscape project: Greencure srl
Dimensions: 31,000 sqm
Costs: 78,000,000 €
Client: Fondazione BEIC
Costs: 20,000,000 €
Client: IULM Università di
Comunicazione e Lingue, REAM sgr

**Project for the nursery school in
the Vado Ligure school complex
(p. 246)**

Scope: international competition, 2023
City: Vado Ligure (Savona), Italy
Status: ongoing, 2023–under
construction
Architectural project: Peluffo & Partners
Dimensions: 360 sqm
Costs: 848,944.80 €
Client: Municipality of Vado Ligure

Peluffo & Partners

Established in 2017
Location: Albissola Marina, Savona. Riviera Italiana

Project team till 2024

Gianluca Peluffo
Architect Founding Partner
Paola De Lucia
Architect Founding Partner, CEO,
Legal Representative
Antonio Lagorio
Architect Founding Partner
Gabriele Filippi
Architect Founding Partner
Domenico Faraco
Architect Founding Partner
Domenica Laface
Architect Founding Partner

Giorgia Console
Architect
Alberto Gaglio
Architect
Stefania Di Adamo
Architect
Giorgia Castelli
Architect Project Manager

Luca Finocchiaro
Construction and Project Manager
Andrea Pepe
Structural Engineering Coordinator

Rina D'urso
Architect and Tender Manager
Francesca Ferrari
Architect
Camillo Leone
Architect
Lucrezia Piervincenzi
Architect
Laura Barducci
Architect
Giulia Sgrò
Architect
Jacopo Peri
Architect

Delfina Bronzi
Office Management and Administration

Adriano Bocca
Art and Culture Manager
Massimo Raciti
Project Manager for Foreign Projects

Previous Collaborators:
Gloria Bernardi
Marco De Petris
Domenico Falci
Maria Isabella Gallo
Sylvie Garrone
Quinn Giroux
Arianna Longo
Eugenia Murialdo
Lidia Nario
Michele Santarelli
Daniela Schiappacasse
Beatrice Teresi
Giulia Tubelli
Jana Van Der Hoeven

Forma Edizioni srl
Florence, Italy
redazione@formaedizioni.it
www.formaedizioni.it

EDITORIAL DIRECTOR
Laura Andreini

EDITORIAL STAFF
Maria Giulia Caliri
Monica Giannini
Beatrice Papucci

PROMOTION AND MARKETING
Stefano Baldassarri
Giulia Di Stefano

TRANSLATIONS
Marlene Klein

PHOTOLITHOGRAPHY
Forma Edizioni

GRAPHIC DESIGN AND LAYOUT
Peluffo & Partners

TEXTS
Valerio Paolo Mosco

ISBN 9 788855 211949
© 2024 Forma Edizioni S.r.l. / Florence, Italy

First edition: December 2024

Gli autori ringraziano: Laura Andreini,
Ernesta Caviola, Maria Fontana di Archivio
Ghirri, Barbara Ghi, Rossella Sileno di
Direzione Regionale Musei Nazionali Toscana
e tutta la redazione di Forma.

First printed in December 2024
by ABC Tipografia, Calenzano, Italy